SPEAKING GAME

"7-Figure Speaker Secrets Revealed"
• Make More Money • Have More Fun
• Conquer Your Fear of Public Speaking
• Become the Confident & Charismatic Person
You've Always Wanted To Be!

CLINT ARTHUR

"SPEAKING GAME"
7-Figure Speaker Secrets Revealed, Conquer Your Fear of Public Speaking, Make More Money, Have More Fun, Become the Confident & Charismatic Person You've Always Wanted To Be!

For REPRINT RIGHTS, BULK SALES, to book Clint Arthur as a SPEAKER for your Conference, or other COMMERCIAL ENQUIRIES CONTACT:

Clint Arthur
5348 Vegas Dr.
Las Vegas, NV 89108
(310)415-0450
www.ClintArthur.TV

"The Real Thing"
- Dan S. Kennedy
The Millionaire Maker

"My Secret Weapon"
- Lisa Sasevich
The Queen of Sales Conversion

"Tripled My Sales"
- Mike Koenigs
You Everywhere Now

"Clint Arthur has done things in the speaking profession no other speaker I have ever heard of or met has been able to do. This book is packed with example stories and illustrations from the Real World that can take your speaking to an even higher level, help you earn more money, and transform you into a charismatic communicator"
- Joel Weldon
National Speaker's Association Hall of Fame

*"Extreme VIP Speaker Training with Clint Arthur
makes you feel like you can do anything!"*
- Dr. Deb Bingham
Functional Medicine Doctor

*"The most transformational training day of my
entire career as a speaker."*
- Alan Kifer
Top Gun Navigator Financial Advisor

BEFORE WE EVEN START, LET'S ELIMINATE ANY INSECURITY YOU MAY HAVE ABOUT PUBLIC SPEAKING, ONCE AND FOR ALL!

One of my clients starred in a movie with Elvis Presley. She and her identical twin sister shared the silver screen with The King in "Double Trouble," and when it came time for cameras to roll she confided to the biggest superstar in the world: "I'm nervous!"

Elvis looked her cold in the eyes and said, "Honey, every time I go on stage I get them butterflies in my stomach — that just means you're alive!"

If Elvis Presley could get nervous before going on stage, I say every mortal being has a right — indeed should expect — to get butterflies, nerves, stage fright, performance anxiety, jitters or whatever you want to call it. You should expect it!

Bruce Springsteen has famously said he would quit performing if he ever stopped getting butterflies before going on stage.

So now that you know the big secret shared by **two** of the biggest stars of all time, here's how to use it to conquer your stage fright, fear of public speaking, jitters or anything else that holds you back when you SPEAK:

Stories
Practice
Energy
Awareness
Keep talking!

Stories are the only thing that everyone wants. Tell stories about your life, about your kids, about your pets, about famous people. Just tell stories. Everybody loves listening to stories. Make it easy, tell real stories you really know because they happened to you!

Practice is essential for anyone who wants to become a better speaker. All professional performers practice, rehearse and refine their "material." People don't like practicing because you "suck" when you practice; but if you don't suck when you practice you will suck when you perform. All great speakers Practice.

Energy is an essential element of good speaking. The easiest way to have good energy is to speak **louder** and **faster**. Speak loud so they hear you, and speak faster so they don't get bored.

Awareness that you have no guarantees that you will wake up tomorrow; this could be the last public speech of your life, so give it all you've got. Put your heart and soul into your performance, and give everything you've got to your audience because this could be the last time you ever get to make your unique difference in the world!

Keep talking — no matter what happens, just keep moving your lips and keep moving your message towards the point you want to make or the end of the story. If you make a mistake, **do not stop**. Nobody knows you made a mistake, and nobody cares as long as you continue entertaining them and keep the performance moving.

My last piece of advice for anyone with a fear of public speaking is that there is nobody pointing a gun at you, and no matter how "horribly you bomb," nobody is going to shoot you for it. If you are persistent and keep trying, and if you keep getting up in front of people and flapping your lips, you will eventually get better and you will make progress and grow as a speaker and as a human being.

Speak! You are the only one who can do it for you!

"6-Figures in 60 Minutes"

30% of the people in this room enrolled in Clint's $1500 TV Publicity Online Group Training

–

It Does NOT Have To Be Perfect!

FOREWORD

Being an effective, powerful, and entertaining speaker is the best thing you can do for your career and your personal power.

IN this special 7-Figure Speaker Training "experience" (complete with videos you can get free at www.SpeakingGame.com) I'm going to deliver to you the lowest hanging fruit, the easiest stuff you can implement today and forever to get better results from your speaking. These tips, tricks and techniques will help you have more impact, influence and income as a result of what you say and *how you say it.*

Speaking is a skill that can be learned and improved. It is one that must be practiced, rehearsed, worked at alone, with other people, in private rooms, on stages, at dinner tables, in conference rooms, anywhere and everywhere you get an opportunity to speak.

Congratulations on the commitment you've made by buying this book — and have FUN!

- Clint Arthur

"People will pay you more for WHO
you are than WHAT you actually do."

Contents

WELCOME TO THE
SPEAKING GAME

WHAT IS...

This book and the BONUS Training Videos at www.SpeakingGame.com will help you maximize your impact, your level of influence, and your actual income by positioning yourself and performing as "someone special." The more "special" people think you are, the more they are going to pay you. You can and must become more special in the eyes of your customers and prospects if you want to make Those Illusive Big Bucks.

I congratulate you for investing your money and especially your time in this training. If you really want to achieve outstanding success and recognition in any field, it takes time and effort. This investment of your time and effort in improving your speaking is going to pay off in spades, because you do it every day, and nobody else you will meet in your "regular life" is studying how to speak, so this will set you apart from and above *everyone*.

...THE SPEAKING GAME?

As PART of this "7-Figure Speaker Training," you're going to learn The Speaking Game. Every waking minute of your life can be much more fun if you make SPEAKING into a game. The whole purpose of The Speaking Game is to make your life more fun, and to make it more fun for your "audience" — whether you are speaking to your child, your coworkers, your boss, ten people in a board room, 100 people in a conference room, a thousand people in a theater, or even 10,000 people in an arena — as many of my students do every day.

Like my great mentor, Dan Kennedy, the best thing I've ever done for myself was to become good at public speaking. Power is unconsciously handed to the person who "steps up" and communicates with confidence, skill, and entertainment value built into their performance. That's why speaker training is so important. Your ability to excel as a speaker is going to massively differentiate you from everybody else.

You may not want people to give you money when you speak; you may just want them to take an action. Getting people to give you money is probably one of the hardest things to get a person to do. If you can get people to give you money you can probably get them to do just about anything. That's why I'm teaching this, because I know how to get people to hand me money immediately after I speak, which is harder than just about anything— and I'm better at it than 99% of the National Speakers Association.

Clint Arthur & Dan Kennedy

"The best thing I've ever done for myself was becoming good at public speaking.
- DAN S. KENNEDY

WHO ARE YOU —

AND WHY SHOULD I CARE?

THAT'S PROBABLY WHAT

YOU'RE THINKING

RIGHT NOW!

THAT IS THE QUESTION

EVERYBODY ASKS THEMSELVES,

EVERY DAY,

ABOUT EVERYONE THEY MEET

"WHO ARE YOU, AND WHY SHOULD I CARE?"

THAT'S the first question people think to themselves. As a Speaker, you **have to** answer that question.

The first section of this training is all about answering that question in a **fast** and *powerful* way, because you have to answer it in a nanosecond.

The most powerful way to answer that question is by <u>*the way*</u> you answer that question. *How you are saying what you say is always more important than what you actually say.* If you say something in a way that's fun and entertaining, or powerful or commanding, you capture a person's interest even if you have no credibility. So how you answer the question is more important — than what you actually say in the answer.

HIGH STATUS
BEGINS
WITH YOUR
FULL NAME

Your credibility, your positioning, your "specialness" begins with your **FULL NAME**

MOST people introduce themselves by saying, "My name is Joe" or "My name is Kathy." On the most basic level, that's reason enough for why you should do something else. In order to be special you need to stand out from the crowd. If everyone just uses their first name, that's a great reason to use your full name.

Important people generally use their full name. If Bill Clinton called and left a voicemail message for you on your answering machine, he would say, "Hey, this is Bill Clinton. I'm going to be in Atlanta this weekend. I want to come to your corporation and do a presentation for a million dollars. Please call my secretary."

He'd never say, "This is Bill." He would always use his full name because he knows that Bill Clinton is the brand, and your personal brand is everything. If you have a personal brand and nobody knows who you are, your personal brand is worth zero. If a lot of people know who you are, then your personal brand is worth a lot.

The goal of being a VIP speaker is to raise your personal brand value. The first, simplest, easiest way is by using your full name. Saying your full name means you think your name is important — you must think you're important if you want other people to.

CREDIBILITY

WHEN you are a speaker at an event there will be a photo of you in a program, or on the website or in some publication that describes who the speakers are. Your credibility has to begin in that photo and your accompanying "bio."

One of the most powerful ways to position yourself as someone special is by using a photo of you from the media. That gives you a third-party endorsement as somebody special. Very often my head shot will be a photograph of me taken out of a media appearance that I've done.

AWARDS

YOU should feature awards you have won, because very few people actually win awards. I took a frame out of my TV appearance on *The Today Show* and used it on my business card, but not just the frame itself. I superimposed a Gold Medal Image of the award I won from GKIC, *Info-Marketer of the Year*. That's a strategy one of my mentors, Jonathan Sprinkles, taught me. When you win an award, create a graphic image for the award to use in your marketing.

AWARDS

ARE

MARKETING

OPPORTUNITIES

BESTSELLER

Most things in business and life these days are primarily *opportunities* to boost your marketing. If you're a **bestselling author these days**, it's mostly about being able to SAY you're a **bestselling author**. I often print on the front cover of my book that I had another book which was a bestseller. On *this* book cover I listed TWO of my previous bestsellers!

#1 INTERNATIONAL BESTSELLER

CLINT ARTHUR

WHAT THEY TEACH YOU AT THE WHARTON BUSINESS SCHOOL

NOTES FROM A STREET-SMART ENTREPRENEUR

WINNER
INFO-MARKETER
OF THE YEAR

My very first Bestselling book — still as relevant as ever!

CREDENTIALS
(DR., PHD, ESQ.)

If you have an impressive
credential,
you are missing out on the
value of that marketing
asset if you don't
USE IT!

If you're a doctor, or a Ph.D. or an attorney, use your credential.

Kim Curtis, CFP®, CHFC®, CLU®, CAP®, AEP®, MSFS

AWARD-WINNING SPEAKER

IF YOU HAVE WON ANY AWARDS AS A SPEAKER YOU SHOULD SAY SO IN YOUR BIO AND WHEN YOU INTRODUCE YOURSELF. AWARDS ARE PRIMARILY USEFUL FOR MARKETING PURPOSES.

FREQUENT SPEAKER

If you're not an award-winning

speaker, you should at least be a

PLACE POWER

Where You Speak Matters

When you watch the videos accompanying this book, you will see that I begin this program by saying: "Welcome to CNN Center in Atlanta." I mention where I filmed the program because it actually *adds value* to the program.

If we were in a hotel in Hoboken I wouldn't say: "Welcome to the Marriott in Hoboken, New Jersey" because there's no status attached to that. But if we're at CNN World Headquarters, there is value to that. Not as much value as if I were to say "Welcome to Harvard," but I want you to know that I have given this exact message and this exact program at Harvard. I have also delivered it to the leaders of America's future at West Point.

One of my mentors, Brendon Burchard, taught me this. He always says, "I've had the great privilege of sharing my message on the same stage as Sir Richard Branson and the Dalai Lama, and at great corporations like GE, Accenture, and Amazon." He makes that statement every time he speaks. I call that *a million-dollar positioning statement.*

Those are prestige speaking engagements. The first one was where he spoke on the same stage as Sir Richard Branson and the Dalai Lama. The next prestige speaking engagements were when Brendon spoke at prestigious places: G.E. Accenture and Amazon. Why are those prestigious? Because you know who those famous men are, and you know what those famous corporations are. You know what Amazon is, and you think that if Brendon spoke at GE or at Amazon he must be somebody amazing, otherwise those major corporations wouldn't have paid him what you imagine must have been *high fees* to come and speak to them.

You want to

speak in

prestigious

places, to

prestigious clients.

If you have

prestigious clients

you should use

their names &

list them in your bio.

PRESTIGE CLIENTS

ONE of my clients is Lisa Sasevich. She's quite a big deal on the Experts Industry seminar circuit, and holds her own seminars attended by hundreds of people at a time. Whenever I speak, I say her name to add prestige to my positioning by virtue of who SHE is. If YOU have prestige clients you should use their names to do the same for YOU.

My client Kim Curtis isn't allowed to say the names of her prestige clients. So, the positioning statement I came up with for her to use is: "My clients include multiple governors of states, national television personalities, and even cage fighting superstars in the UFC." Each category of client is "prestigious" (or at least "outstanding.") Governors of states, national television personalities, UFC superstars — these are all seemingly prestigious things. *You need to come up with a way to describe who your clients are that positions you as a more important person, based on **their** status and prestige.*

NUMBER
OF CLIENTS

"Billions and billions served." You've read those words on signs in front of McDonald's restaurants thousands...

...of times in your life. "Billions and billions served." That is no error, and it is very impressive. It makes them seem like they're special. That's why my clients and I use big numbers to infer or create HIGH STATUS positioning.

Our 2015 Event Speakers

NUMBER OF YEARS

USING numbers of years is one of my favorite tricks. Dan Kennedy's been a professional speaker for more than 42 years. *He must know a lot if he's been doing it for more than 42 years.*

And you know what? If you've been in business for decades, you must know something too, because most businesses fail within the first five years! If you've been able to persist for that long you must've learned a few things, and there must be something special about you — which is the purpose of Positioning.

One of the people who attended my training session introduced himself and said, "I'm the author of a book that has touched over 100,000 lives. Over the past decade I've made over a million dollars. And now I teach ordinary people just like you to skip the rat race and achieve financial freedom."

Let's break his statement apart and look at it closely: "Over the past decade I've made more than one million dollars." That actually works against him. Making a hundred thousand dollars a year is not going to inspire anyone — so he shouldn't say "over the past decade." He should say, "I made more than a million dollars selling information online," or whatever statement omits the unimpressive part. The number of years you've been in business is helpful and impressive—unless it took you a long time to make money. If you're going to be bragging about making money, then you want to say that you made the money fast.

"

HEY!

"

THIS IS SOMETHING <u>NO ONE ELSE</u> WILL TEACH YOU. There's not another person in the entire world who teaches the power of saying "Hey."

You would never say "hey" to the Pope. It's very difficult to say "hey" to the President of the United States.

I recently met Bill Clinton and Hillary Clinton. This was incredibly interesting, because when you meet major celebrities, your true level of personal power will come out, and what the true power situation is will reveal itself. It's very hard for you to control it unless you do it a lot. And even though I meet major celebrities more often than most people, I am fascinated by what occurred when I met Bill Clinton and Hillary Clinton.

I was at my daughter's graduation ceremony from USC Film School. Hillary's nephew Zachary Rodham was also in the graduating class. The Clintons were in the front row, so I went down near the front because I wanted to get a selfie with them. As soon as I sat down, Bill Clinton stood up and started walking up the aisle towards me.

I stood and fell into step with him, and this is exactly what came out of my mouth: "Sir, can I get a photo?" Bill Clinton has tremendous personal power and authority. Did I say "Hey Bill, can I get a photo?" No. I said, "Sir, can I get a photo?"

He didn't object, so I quickly snapped a selfie of us. I was so excited I rushed to show it to my family. They were blown away!

About an hour later, as the ceremony was wrapping up, I thought, *Hillary is going to be leaving soon — I'm going to get a photo with Hillary too!* I moved to a seat near where they were sitting, and sure enough, within minutes they both stood up and started walking toward me — on the other side of a velvet rope.

I approached the rope and spoke up over the growing thrum of voices in the auditorium: "Hey Hillary, can I get a picture?" Those were my exact words.

In a very sarcastic way she said, "Sure!" So I leaned over the velvet rope and snapped my selfie; and that's exactly how I got my picture with Hillary Clinton.

The word "hey" is powerful because it's hard to say "hey" to somebody who is more powerful than you. As a reverse engineer, I take what's there, and work backwards from the end result to see what's really going on. It's hard to say "hey" to someone who's more powerful than you, but it's easy to say hey to somebody at your level or below. For example, if my dog was scratching on the wall, to stop my dog scratching on the wall I'd just say "Hey!"

So ultimately, if you want to be a VIP Speaker — someone with a lot of "game" — you want to be viewed as being more powerful, more special, different and better than others, and you should say "Hey" all the time, especially when you start speaking your positioning statement. For example, when I introduced myself, I say "Hey, I'm Clint Arthur."

When you say "hey," you want to do it in a way that people don't notice that you're actually being rude.

I think that may be why Hillary Clinton answered me the way she did. She didn't consciously realize what I was doing, but on a subconscious level she understood the subtext of my words, and therefore she gave me that kind of sarcastic, flip answer. Certainly "hey" is disrespectful when you compare it to saying "sir," when I got my selfie with Bill Clinton.

"Hey" is a super-powerful word, and you should use it all the time as a tool in positioning yourself.

HOW TO SAY 'HEY'

The ideal way to use the word "hey" is to sound as if you're talking to a friend. Many times, you'll call up a friend and say "Hey, what's going on?" They know it's you by your voice.

Saying "hey" is a casual thing, said by peers.

Or you'll say to your child, "Hey, get over here!" or "Hey, get away from that!" It's also a word used by a superior — and a word that makes an assumption of power in the relationship. So when you use the word "hey," the most effective way — potentially the least offensive way — to use the word is to say it as if you're the person's friend.

So, for example, when I was doing a VIP speaker training session last year, I knew that I had to call up a TV producer before she got off work. I said to my class, "Hey guys, let me just take five minutes and make a call." I did a cold call where I called a TV producer I had never talked to, and pitched her on the phone. This is exactly the way it went:

First, I called the news desk, and the person answering the phone said, "News."

I said, "Hey, is Lisa there?" That's exactly what I said, in a vey casual and friendly way.

The person at the news desk said, "Sure, hang on a second." He thought I was one of Lisa's *friends*.

Then Lisa picked up the phone: "This is Lisa."

"Hey Lisa, are you the producer who books the guests?" Now she knows that it's not her friend calling. She knows who her friends are, but what she doesn't know is that now *I've grabbed the power.* "<u>Hey</u> Lisa, are you the producer who books the guests?"

"Yes I am."

She submitted to my "hey" — I grabbed the power. The most important people on TV are the people who are on TV, not the people behind the scenes. Although the people behind the scenes have the most power, if there was no person on the show, there would be no show. The show is all driven by the talent: hosts, anchors, guests, and by the celebrities who go on TV shows.

If you are a celebrity on a show you're more important than the producer. The producer may think in their conscious mind that they are more important than you, but they know on a subconscious level that if you weren't there, there would be no show. If the producer could be on the show, on camera, they would be — but they can't. If the producer could be the one on camera they would do it. They would grab the power. The producer knows that a celebrity is more important than they are, so a producer is willing to take the insult from a celebrity.

And if they're willing to take it, you should give it to them. You should insult them. You should grab the power, because if you don't you're not being true to your role in the power hierarchy. This is my reverse engineering of the situation. You have to act the way you're supposed to act or else you're not who you want to be.

If the most powerful person in the room can insult other people, they should, but they must do it in a friendly way to camouflage the insult. That's why I asked, "Hey Lisa, are you the producer who books the guests?"

Consciously, the other person shouldn't even realize that I've grabbed the power, but it <u>does</u> register on a subconscious level.

I was critical of Donald Trump's *performances* in a lot of his speeches during his "Thank You Tour" after the 2016 election, so I made a training video for Donald Trump. I do believe that he watched my video, because he has transformed his performances exactly the way I instructed him to in the training. I deliberately started that video with the word "hey." It was easier for me to do it because he <u>wasn't</u> in the room: I was just

IF YOU'RE SUPPOSED TO BE THE MOST POWERFUL PERSON IN THE ROOM YOU HAVE TO ACT LIKE...

making a video. But I very deliberately started my scripted presentation: "Hey, I'm Clint Arthur." I used "hey" to grab power.

I want you to respect the fact that I'm spending a lot of time on "hey." It's that powerful. At Celebrity Launchpad I guarantee my students that they will book themselves on at least three TV shows, and the word "hey" is a huge part of that training because it's so powerful.

At a recent training session, I had the students practice introducing themselves. One student started by saying "good morning, my name is..." "Hey" is much more powerful. "Good morning?" What does that say about you? It says *I want you to like me*. "Good morning" is what a people pleaser says. When you say "hey," people think *That is a celebrity.*

...THE MOST POWERFUL PERSON IN THE ROOM, OR ELSE YOU'RE NOT.

YOUR
"WHO ARE YOU, AND WHY SHOULD I CARE?"
STATEMENT

SO now we're going to put it all together into a single solid statement that deals with the question: "Who are you, and why should I care." We're going to go through everything that we just learned and use it in one statement. This will change who you are. I would say it like this.

"Hey, my name is Clint Arthur, number one bestselling author of *What They Teach You at the Wharton Business School*, and *21 Performance Secrets of Donald Trump*. I'm an award-winning speaker and entrepreneur, and I've taught more than 600 authors, speakers, coaches and entrepreneurs how to book themselves on TV for free, resulting in more than 3,524 Network TV bookings that I'm aware of."

Less is always better.

There cannot be a pause between hey and your name. Use your credentials. Every word counts. No extra words!

It is crucially important that you speak clearly. When you enunciate well I can understand what you're saying, I know who you are. If you don't enunciate properly, some people who don't know you won't learn who you are, and they will tune out instead of struggling to listen to what you're saying.

You've seen the power of "hey" and how to introduce yourself powerfully... Now let's go into The Speaking Game. *This is how you turn Speaking into a Game!*

VOICE TRICKS

The Speaking Game is primarily about your voice. It's also about the content, and to an extent, about your marketing as a speaker. But on the most fundamental levels it's about your voice.

WHAT can you do with your voice? You can engage people, grab their attention, captivate them, and influence them to do what you want.

Let's start with how you score points in The Speaking Game — and through this process, you'll learn how to have more impact, more influence, and make more income.

VOLUME

THE first thing you can do with your voice is to change the volume. This is the easiest way to score points in the game, and to have more impact when you speak.

When you think about a person who is a great speaker, you might describe them as a dynamic speaker. What does the word "dynamic" mean? The word dynamic means "change." So if you want to be a dynamic speaker, deconstruct what that really means, and do what you have to do. That means you are going to change things about the quality of your voice. The easiest thing you can change is your volume.

So now, *practice changing your volume*. You've got to be clearly loud, and clearly soft. You can do this without even using words:

In stead of words, say:
A,B,C,D,E,F,G,H,I,J,K,L,M,N,O,P...

SPEED

THE second way to win points in The Speaking Game is to vary your speed. Sometimes you should talk really fast, and sometimes speak really slow.

When practicing, use both speeds, then come back to your original speed to really demonstrate that you have control. Talk really fast right, then talk really slow, then go back to talking really fast again.

A lot of times it's easier really to work on these techniques without using actual words. If you're not clear about what you're going to say, it's always easier to say "blah blah blah blah" when you practice

You demonstrate your mastery of the topic by going slow, slow, slow and then going fast fast fast. Make everything clear and crisp.

When you see a professional athlete, like a professional boxer, have you ever watched how fast they punch? Super fast! Go to a baseball game and watch the players throw a baseball around the outfield. Even when the guys are just warming up, they whip that ball around SOOOO fast. Or basketball players, passing the ball between themselves. Professional athletes pass the ball *fast!* Pro speakers can talk really fast, really fast, and then slow. So you should talk slowly, and then talk really fast. Add Variety.

SUSTAIN

The next way to score points in The Speaking Game is by sustaining a word.

Sometimes, if you want to emphasize your point, you just sustaaaaaaaaain a word.

This creates drama.

PAUSE

The…

pause

…is another very dramatic way to win points in The Speaking Game.

It's a very powerful and easy way to inject…

drama

…into your message.

STARS

END UP

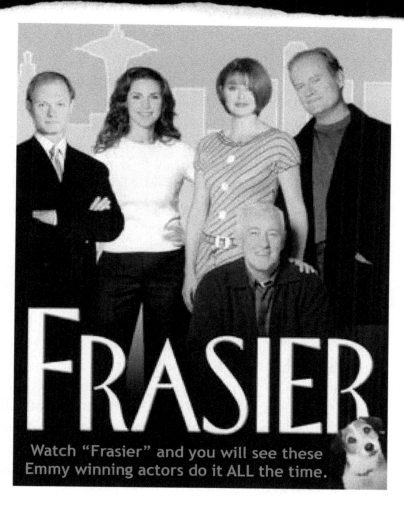

FRASIER

Watch "Frasier" and you will see these Emmy winning actors do it ALL the time.

"Hollywood's BIG Secrets"

These are the 2 biggest success secrets in Hollywood, and 2 of my most important 7-Figure VIP speaking tricks:

1) After graduating from The Wharton Business School, I pursued the Hollywood dream for 13 years, the last six of which were particularly rough — as I spent much of my time behind the wheel of a taxi. This caused no end of embarrassment to my father, an accountant whose greatest pride and joy was that I'd graduated from Wharton.

One night my dad took me out to dinner at Angelo & Maxie's Steakhouse on Park Avenue South in Manhattan — a Seriously Great New York City steakhouse in the 1990's.

In the middle of the dinner, I spotted my dad's best friend, Danny Lembo across the restaurant. Perpetually tan and in great shape, Dan was a finalist on *Survivor Nicaragua*, as well as Executive Vice President of an Amex-listed REIT — and when he spots me across the dining room he comes bounding up to the table with a huge grin and bellows: "Look who it is — the Wharton taxi driver!" *Poor dad shriveled!*

During my starving artist odyssey, I studied acting with Howard Fine, at the Howard Fine Acting Studio.

Who is Howard Fine
— And Why Should I Care?

I met my daughter's mother at the Sundance Film Festival about 7 years into what turned out to be my Hollywood Nightmare. This was right around the time that George Clooney became a huge star on "ER" — she had been George Clooney's agent for 10 years. About a month after we started dating, (and 2 months before she got pregnant with our daughter) she said, "if you want to be an actor in Hollywood you have to study with Howard Fine. All the up and coming actors study with Howard Fine."

So I pulled out my credit card and went to the Howard Fine Acting Studio. In one of the early classes, Howard Fine gave you us all a line and told us to come up on the stage and say the line. If you said the line correctly he said "yes!" — if you said it incorrectly he said "no."

Student after student went up on stage and said the line: "The fault, Dear Brutus, lies not in our stars, but in ourselves, that we are underlings." He groaned "No" after "No" after "No," — then finally Howard Fine said "Yes!" I never understood why, and he never explained why. That's the shortcoming of the Howard Fine method, at least as it was in those days. He wouldn't even explain to you what you did wrong or how to do it right either — because this is the big success secret of Hollywood actors.

The biggest secret in Hollywood! The difference between winners and losers in Hollywood is this one simple trick. Deconstruct it. Deconstruct who's winning Emmy Awards, who's winning Academy Awards, and who's driving taxis, and the answer comes down to this secret.

Stars End Up!

Go to SpeakingGame.com NOW for FREE Training on Ending Up

The final inflection in their voice is not down – it's up!

When you say your name, end *up*. The last syllable should have a rising note. Everything you say should end *up*. It makes what you say much more interesting. On a deeper level, it helps the audience to actually hear what you're saying, because if you don't end up, you end down. And if you end down, the tendency is to just dribble your words out. When you end *up* it gives energy to the very last syllable.

You have to give energy all the way through your thought —
and if you don't go *up* then you're probably going to go down
— and it's much more powerful to go up because **it's easier to
hear you!**

Be Present!

2) The other big secret to being a Hollywood TV or Movie
star is *being present in the moment.* TV and Movie stars are
more present in the moment, that's why they're more
interesting to watch. When you *end up* it forces you to be
present in the moment all the way through to the end of your
thought. That's full presence. As a speaker you want to be
fully present during every word of your speech.

If you can do that you will become a tremendous speaker,
because most people are not prisoners, and they don't have to
listen if they don't want to. In fact, most people are on their
phone, texting somebody in another state — that's how "not
present" they are. Most people are in their head, thinking
about what they're going to say three seconds from now.
They can't even be present in this moment, because they're
too worried about being present three seconds from now to
be present right now. So if you force yourself into the
discipline of pronouncing your words *up,* it forces you to be
present in each and every moment of every word.

Another thing: Turn your phone off. Again, *be present in this
moment.* You can learn a lot more by being fully present right
now than you will by responding to any text messages, or e-
mails from random people trying to grab your attention. So
turn off your phone, and really be present as you read this
book.

Are you uncomfortable? Are you out of your comfort zone?
As I said on *The Today Show,* life begins where your comfort
zone ends. [Watch Brooke Shields interview the author of
this book on *The Today Show* at www.SpeakingGame.com]

THE HIGH-LOW GAME: A GAME *WITHIN* THE SPEAKING GAME

THIS game was taught to me by one of my mentors, the great and powerful genius, the wonderful person, the superstar voice teacher, Roger Love. His clients include Tony Robbins, Stevie Wonder, et cetera. Roger Love really knows how to speak and perform like a champion, and he's the one who taught me The High-Low Game.

The High-Low Game is about melody, and the way you play is that sometimes you use low notes, and sometimes you use high notes. Make your voice go low and high, low and high, and the more you can make your voice go low and go high, and low and high, the more success you have with The High-Low Game—injecting more melody into your voice.

This is about forcing you to have more range in your voice. You want to have low notes and you want to have medium notes, and you want to have high notes. And you want medium and low, and high and low, and high and medium. That's what it's all about. It's going to force you to develop more range in your voice. And believe me when I tell you, *I have created my voice*. People say I have a great voice. I had a *good* voice before I started doing all this stuff.

I have developed my vocal range, and I've developed my ability to speak in lower tones, in the lower register of my voice. In the private members area of my Celebrity Launchpad web site, I have a video called "Clint Arthur on Better TV." In that video I'm walking up Third Avenue in New York City, doing vocal exercises, deliberately training my voice in the lower range — because when you get nervous there is a tendency for your voice to go higher.

As a speaker, you don't want to seem nervous. You want to come off *cool*. So how do you come off as cool? Again, deconstructing it, *a high voice indicates that you're nervous and a low voice indicates that you're cool.*

So I have deliberately, systematically, methodically trained my voice in the lower register, and you can do that too. Now, with that said, I also deliberately and very often utilize a high, squeaky falsetto voice for dramatic effect.

You want to use as much of your arsenal of vocal abilities as you possibly can to add as much dynamic range into your presentations as you can.

The more you use these tools, the more you use these skills and develop these powers, the more comfortable you will be when you do, and the less awkward it will feel to you when you're speaking.

A lot of times I'll really mix it up, for emphasis — and to blow people's minds — because people are not used to hearing aggressive use of this high low strategy. And when you start mixing it up like that you can go high, and you can really hit on the high notes, which wakes the listeners up. *That's your minimum job as a speaker: keep the audience awake!*

The usual monotone delivery gets a make-over when you work on your range. You might be surprised, but a lot people talk using only one note. I would imagine that most of your life you talk using one or just a few notes. There's no reason to be restricted.

Mastery of The Speaking Game transforms your speaking and everything you say. Not only does it become more fun to speak, but you also gain total freedom, because you realize that no matter what you say, and no matter how it comes out, it is perfectly fine — just as long as you play the game. And the more unexpected, the more your voice surprises you, the better it is. And if you're constantly surprising yourself, that's total freedom!

SECRETS

OF

GREAT

PERFORMANCE

Performance

SECRETS of

Donald Trump

Whether you love him or hate him, as someone who wants to be a better speaker, you must realize Donald Trump became president of the United States for two reasons:

First and foremost, he's a fantastic speaker. He really does know how to speak. He uses all kinds of tricks. In this section, we're going to look at some of the biggest tricks Donald Trump uses when he speaks.

The second reason why Donald Trump became president of the United States is his use of what I call Mega Media. He makes TV appearances, and they get posted on social media. That's using "old media" and "new media" to create what I call Mega Media. When you repurpose TV onto social media it becomes mega media. TV has more status than social media. Everybody, anybody, can be on social media. As Veronica Grey, one of my earliest TV clients so perfectly put it, "YouTube is the great equalizer. Television is the great separator."

So, when you take the media that separates celebrities from the masses, and you use it on social media, it empowers social media like nothing else you can do. Today, you have to use social media if you really want to have an impact. But if you use TV in your social media, your social media presence is going to be more powerful than people who don't use TV.

LET'S TAKE A LOOK AT PERFORMANCE SECRETS OF DONALD TRUMP >>>

STATUS

SECRET #1

Dan Kennedy "used to speak in the arenas at Success Seminars with Donald Trump," and Dan says that *an entrepreneur's number one job is to raise their status*.

Celebrity attachment and place attachment are definite strategies that Donald Trump uses: famous people's names, our alma matter's name, the Wharton Business School; and speakers attach their name to Harvard all the time. This is a deliberate strategy of celebrity and place attachment.

Every entrepreneur should be using the same exact technique. This is not namedropping for the sake of vanity. This is a deliberate strategy to raise his status in the eyes of customers and prospect, and we can all take a lesson from Donald Trump on this technique of using high-status words when we speak.

This naturally leads into a discussion on content. I believe that as somebody who wants to appear to be more special — of higher status than your customers, prospects, or competition — you should deliberately use "status language" in the form of celebrity names and famous high-status places.

As you will see when you watch the free videos at www.SpeakingGame.com, when I gave this training in a live presentation, I started by saying "we're here at CNN Center today to film this program," adding status and power to the presentation. If we were across the park at the Westin I wouldn't say it, but we were at CNN, so I used the power of the CNN brand.

You as a speaker should be using famous people's names. It's the easiest thing you can do to raise the status and power of your "content."

I've mentioned Donald Trump's name several times already. A lot of people don't talk about famous people. They just don't use the names of famous people in their presentations. Why not? It's something you can do just by deciding to do it. It's completely free, and it completely changes the impact of your words and your whole presentation. People start to think, *Does he know Donald Trump? Does he know Hillary Clinton? Does he know Bill Clinton?* I met Bill Clinton and Hillary Clinton at my daughter's college graduation a couple of weeks ago. I took selfies with them. But you wouldn't know it unless I told you. You make assumptions. That's what people do, they *assume* things.

I use those pictures on my professional web site. When you go to www.ClintArthur.TV you see the pictures of me with famous people. Those pictures change how you see me. Every time you use the name of a famous person in your presentation, you score a point in The Speaking Game.

For example, Oprah, Michael Jackson, Lady Gaga, Donald Trump, Warren Buffett, Barack Obama, George Washington, Abraham Lincoln, Colin Powell, Albert Einstein — that's 10 points in The Speaking Game! How easy was that? The whole goal of The Speaking Game is to get to 100. Play alone, to improve your speaking skills, or with friends. Whoever gets to 100 first wins!

Imagine that you're at a party with friends, and you just want to have fun, so you say, "Hey, let's play The Speaking Game." Start keeping score for yourself, and drop in enough celebrity names, play the Hi-Lo game, speak softer and louder, softer and louder, insert a strategic pause, speak faster and slower — you get a lot of points from doing that. And the first person to get to 100 points wins the game.

The easiest way to win the game is with high status language.

For example, I've already said in this presentation, "This is exactly what I taught when I spoke at Harvard," or "when I spoke at West Point." That's two points right there. It's powerful! And most people don't do it. They don't know enough to do it.

Why does Donald Trump do it? Because it works. He does it all the time. And who's the 45th president of the United States? Him. That's ultimate proof that it works. *Status language is the first Secret of Donald Trump's success.*

LET'S MOVE ON TO THE SECOND SECRET...

ENERGY

Secret #2

Donald Trump used the importance of ENERGY as a powerful weapon during the 2016 Presidential Campaign, against Jeb Bush, against Hillary Clinton, and even against (the status quo) Barack Obama.

Speaking is all about energy. Energy comes off as confidence, and you need confidence if you want to be president of the United States — or if you want to sell anything. Selling is a transference of confidence.

Donald Trump knows all about energy, and he understands deliberate strategies you can use to convey more energy. Speaking fast and speaking loudly make it seem that you have more energy.

Hand gestures are another great way to inject energy into your speaking. We can do a lot more with our hands than even with our face. Trump comes across with the energy of a 35 year old. His energy is unbelievable!

There are different ways to inject more energy into your performance. I believe that *energy is the essential element of great performance*, because I believe that people are energy vampires. What people really want is energy.

When people go to see a speaker, invariably the speaker who gets the highest ratings is the one who projects the most energy. Why? Let's deconstruct it. *The person who has the most confidence, conviction, and enthusiasm for their topic is perceived to be the best speaker.*

Enthusiasm is energy. When you really want somebody to get something, when you're super enthusiastic about it, other people can feel the energy and the passion in your voice. That's the trick: energy equals enthusiasm.

So how can you project more energy? There are four ways to have more energy. The first way is the easiest way. *Speak louder,* especially on video. If you want to convey more enthusiasm for your topic, **Energy Secret #1 is to SPEAK LOUDER.**

The second way to project more energy is to *speak faster.* If you're a car salesman and you don't earn any money unless you sell a car, you're somebody who knows how to use this trick. You've heard this phrase: "He's like a fast-talking car salesman." There's a reason why car salesmen talk fast: energy. They don't eat unless they sell cars. That's why they are fast-talking car salesmen — talking fast is a trick to convey energy, passion, and enthusiasm.

A lot of people say, "people don't buy products—people buy people." There is a lot of truth to that. When a person buys a product, very often they buy it from another person because that person is confident and conveys confidence about that product. So the **2nd easy way to project more energy is to TALK FASTER!**

The 3rd way to inject more

energy into your speaking is to bounce up and down before you speak. Physically bounce a few inches off the ground, up and down, 10 times before you speak. Physically move your body! This will get your blood pumping and circulating oxygen throughout your body, and oxygen will give you more energy.

The 4th way to get more

energy is to pat all the parts of your body with your fingers and palms. Start by patting the top of one hand with the other hand, then work your way up that arm, all the way to your chest. Then do the same thing with your other hand to your other hand and arm. Then bend over and pat your ankles, calves, knees, thighs, hips, stomach, chest, back, neck and head. Again, this will accelerate your blood flow, but it will also make you more aware of all the parts of your body, and as a result, **make you more present in the moment and more present in your body.**

ENERGY

Louder

Faster

Bounce

Pat

COSTUME

SECRET #3

CLINT ARTHUR
"THE BUTTER MAN"

The third seCret of Donald Trump's success is Costume.

As a performer, remember that *your first responsibility as a speaker is to entertain.* So if you're an entertainer when you're a speaker, you're not a businessman anymore—you're an entertainer. Entertainers don't wear clothes, they wear costumes.

When Steve Jobs was doing keynote presentations at Apple Worldwide Developer Conferences, wasn't speaking like the CEO of Apple. He was an entertainer. That's why he was so successful.

I've read and studied *Performance Secrets of Steve Jobs.* It's why I titled my book *21 Performance Secrets of Donald Trump:* I was modeling it after the huge mega-success of the

Steve Jobs book. Jobs always wore the exact same *costume*. Figure out a costume for yourself and you'll be way ahead of where you would be *without* a costume.

When you're a speaker you are an entertainer, and entertainers wear costumes. What is your costume? You may have to evolve your costume multiple times before you get it right and really hit it and make a huge impact with costume, but it's possible to do it, and you should do it. Do you have enough true desire to get it right?

Be careful about wearing a "wrong" or "bad" costume. One time I watched a female speaker talk for 20 minutes on stage with her great pair of legs barely concealed by a too-short skirt.

After that speech I went up to her and said, "I'm sure you have an important message, but I didn't hear a single word you said because I couldn't stop looking at your legs. So next time you speak you might want to choose a different costume — one that's not so distracting for the audience."

Ultimately, your message is the point, and you must do everything you can to support it, not distract from it.

You and I are speakers because we have a message that we want to share, whether that message is "get better grades in school so you can grow up and have a better life," or "buy this computer software so that you can make more money" — or whatever your message may be.

If people are distracted by the imperfection or the poor choice of your costume, that's going to decrease the effectiveness of your message. If they are not focused on your mouth because your naked flesh is distracting, then your skin is shooting your message in the foot.

REHEARSE

DONALD TRUMP has been doing his act in Arenas for many many years. During the campaign every rally was rehearsal for the next. Those rallies created the opportunity for him to rehearse onstage in front of thousands of people every single day.

Every time he said the line about "building the wall" it got better. I heard him say it in Las Vegas in December 2015; he got a huge ovation from the crowd. Then I heard him again in Reno in February 2016, and the ovation was even bigger. All of this was rehearsal for the big speech in July at the convention.

Professional speakers rehearse. This is why I have my students say "who you are and why we should care" over and over in rehearsal — so that you get used to saying it. The more you say it, the easier it gets to say it under pressure. You should rehearse saying who you are and why we should care a hundred times. Or more, if necessary. Say it, out loud, until you can say it perfectly. Say it until you can ad-lib who you are and why would we should care. You have to be able to use your voice, and

73

use your words, in ways that just *flow,* and rehearsal is the only way to make that happen.

A lot of people don't like to rehearse because they think they sound bad when they rehearse. But the problem is, if you don't sound bad when you rehearse, you *will* sound bad when you perform. When you are speaking in front of an audience or when you are speaking on TV, that's the WRONG time to sound bad!

The time to sound bad is when you rehearse, not when you perform.

The other benefit of rehearsal is iteration. A lot of times people will say, "I'm not ready to come to *Celebrity Launchpad* because I don't have my message all together — my message isn't tight enough for TV!"

How do you get a great message? Through rehearsal and the iteration that comes from rehearsal. Rehearsal for performance develops your messaging. Every time you go on TV is a rehearsal for the next time you're on TV. Each appearance is also rehearsal for the next.

On my first *Mornings With Maria* appearance, I was a little bit tongue-tied. So for my next appearance on that show I got up extra early, and started rehearsing earlier. The next time I was on that show my voice was more warmed up. I only had about an hour and a half of warm-up the first time. The second time I was on the show my hit was at 7:30 a.m., so I got up at 4:30 and had two-and-a-half hours of rehearsal. As a result, my voice and words were flowing better when I was on her show the second time. I did an extra hour of rehearsal because I realized from the first experience that I needed more rehearsal for that caliber of performance environment.

Each time you perform it's a rehearsal for the next time you perform. The iteration of rehearsal is probably the most valuable aspect of rehearsing. There's a great video of me inside the *Celebrity Launchpad* members area called "Clint Arthur on NBC Phoenix." In that video, you see me rehearsing for one of my NBC Phoenix appearances. I'm in the Phoenix Convention Center, about 9:00PM, and I'm walking around all alone in an empty 5000 square foot convention hall. I videotaped a lot of it for the "behind the scenes" video, and that's where I learned the power of rehearsal.

Donald Trump speaks in front of so many audiences that his rehearsals are always public performances. Although, now that he's President, for big speeches like the State of the Union address I hope he rehearses his performance in private, with coaches.

WE need to rehearse in private, and with audiences, whenever we can get them. For us, every public performance is a rehearsal for the next one. And for me, every time I go on TV it's a rehearsal for the next, bigger television appearance.

EXPRESSIONS

PEOPLE thought I was joking when I was on Fox Business Channel and said Donald Trump does crazy facial expressions on purpose.

I'm not joking. He does it on purpose. And *one of the most powerful ways to use your face is to use your eyes in your expressions*.

When I speak, I usually tell this story: When I was 14 years old I made up my mind that I was going to graduate from the Wharton Business School. I thought... *If I could graduate from someplace super special, like Wharton, the best business school in the world—I'll become special, and maybe my parents will stop arguing so much*. You know, when you're a little kid you think everything's your fault.

I graduated from Wharton with a 4.0 GPA in my entrepreneurial management major, and then went to visit my parents. Sure enough, they got into a huge argument, and dad stormed out of the house and slammed the door.

I was sitting on the couch in the living room when I turned to my mom and asked, "The way he resents you all these years—have you been cheating on dad?"

I'm sitting there thinking to myself, *I cannot believe I just asked my mother that question! What kind of a smart-ass kid asks his own mother if she's cheating on his father?* And then I started thinking, *How come she isn't answering the question?*

Finally she said, "He's not your real father. Your real father was a doctor at the fertility clinic, and you look just like him."

Can you imagine? Everything I thought I knew... in a second—*poof!* I didn't know who I was anymore, and I certainly didn't know what I wanted to be when I grew up anymore.

So naturally I told the investment bank on the 87th floor of number 1 World Trade Center, "I'm not interested in your job in investment banking," and I moved out to Hollywood, in search of reinventing who I was — discovering the answer to "who is Clint Arthur?"

I tell that story all the time. And do a huge expression with my eyes wide — I do the expression deliberately. It's a dramatic effect that I put in there because it has an impact, gets laughs. That's the same thing Donald Trump does.

You're not a *person* speaking. You are an *entertainer*, and you have a very powerful tool to use — your eyes. Eye expressions are Super powerful! If you're not using them, you're not using the most powerful tool of your face.

Watch
Clint tell *that* story at
www.SpeakingGame.com

TEETH

SECRET #6

TEETH are part of Donald Trump's secreTs of success. In case you haven't noticed, he's got a full set of white, white, white porcelain veneers in his mouth. White, white teeth.

If you want to be successful as a speaker, you have to learn how to use your teeth. Ideally, you're going to *learn how to smile while you talk.* All the top people on TV smile while they talk. Some women in particular have teeth which are advantageous to them, like Lee Carter (the beautiful and brilliant lady in the red dress my first two times on Fox Business Channel.) She's got a mouthful of great teeth, and it always looks like she's smiling whether she's actually smiling or not; it looks like she's smiling. Some people are lucky like that. I'm not. I've had to develop whatever ability I have to smile and show my teeth while I'm speaking. I trained myself to do it. You can too.

The other part of using your teeth is that even if you're not actually smiling and looking friendly, you should still use teeth in your presentations, just as Donald Trump does.

A lot of times he snarls at the audience or at the cameras with his teeth — like a lion, a mad dog, or a wild animal.

This is strategic use of teeth. It's dramatic and it's very powerful

Why are teeth so powerful? Because teeth are little neon lights in your mouth attracting the viewers' attention.

White teeth maximize the effective use of this strategy, so you should whiten your teeth so that they are white-white-white, or at least whiter! If you can't go the full nine yards and get a full set of porcelain veneers like Donald Trump, or you don't want to, that's ok. But whiten your teeth, because speakers use white teeth to attract the eyes of the viewer.

ZOOM Teeth Whitening is a great solution. Do you have the commitment to do it?

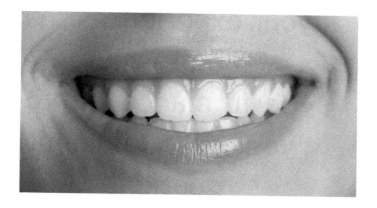

You are somebody.

Be something.

Something is always better than nothing.

Don't be afraid to enhance WHO and WHAT you are by making choices about your teeth, your body, your hair, your costume, your energy level, your words, and your experiences that add to your performance and to your entertainment quotient.

SETTING

SECRET #7

THE final "S" in "SecretS" is for *Setting*.

Donald Trump understands that each presentation is showbiz. To add showbiz to each event, he's a total master of creating powerful and effective Setting.

Let's take a look at some of the settings for Trump rallies. (Google "Trump Rally" and look at the image results.) At every Trump rally there were massive displays of flags; state flags and U.S. flags displayed in rows — and the cloth of the flags was always spread out. Before Trump rallies, I never even noticed that there was such a thing as a flag spreader that spreads the cloth of flags for pretty display. Donald Trump's use of flag spreaders was the first time I ever noticed flags displayed like that.

And there were always "Trump for President" signs. Where did those signs come from? At the beginning of both rallies I attended in person, before Donald Trump came out, his paid staff handed out signs. That's why there were signs at all of the rallies! I have two of them, a blue one and a white one, and the white one says, "The silent majority is for Donald Trump." We got Donald Trump to personally sign that one after the rally.

For his setting, Trump always had signs, red-white-and-blue bunting, black backdrops, flags, and always had a podium that said "Trump." Always.

Hillary Clinton would never do any of this stuff. Hillary Clinton's rallies? It certainly didn't look like you were watching the next president of the United States! And this is not a political message. This is a message about the power of Setting.

My favorite Trump rally was early on, on a battleship. An incredible use of setting. Before the second GOP debate had a rally on a battleship because he knew the setting would give him power.

Deliberate choice of setting is a valuable tool that a speaker can use.

Now the question becomes, "what are you doing with setting?"

For example, I spoke recently at an event called the where I paid $5000 to speak. Onstage they had plants. Why? What did it have to do with anything? I don't know. To me, it was just distracting.

Why would there be a whole forest of ferns behind me when I'm speaking on stage trying to teach? What's the point of that? I don't know. I was just an invited guest. But when you have control of th, set ,you should be very deliberate about what is in the set, because it makes a difference.

HANDS

Donald Trump is very deliberate about his use of hands.

In the piece on Fox Business, Dagen McDowell, the host that day, said "He's got those hands," having fun with the fact that I use my hands a lot on TV.

You should use your hands when you're on TV or any time you speak. It's a very easy way for you to be more expressive in your gestures, and there is more energy in your presentations when you use your hands.

My client, Dr. Mario Torres-Leon, says we actually have 12 hands.

Did you know you've got 12 hands? Each finger is a "hand." Then you have the full hands themselves. So you've got all these hands. Use 'em! If you're not using your hands you're missing out on valuable communication tools.

And using your hands is not just about injecting energy. It could also be about mood. You can do all kinds of things with your hands, and you should! When you're playing The Speaking Game you get points every time you put in some kind of really good hand gesture.

SMILE

Veronica Grey on Good Morning America

THESE are the secrets of powerful speakers, it's all put together for you in a game called The Speaking Game — and every time you smile, you get a point just for a smile. Why not just score a point by smiling as many times as you can? It' so easy! (It's actually not, but it should be!)

Here's a very interesting thing: this is how I learned that a smile is worth a point. I was a judge at a beauty contest, and it was a fascinating experience because nobody told me how to score. I just made it up.

The contestants entered from stage left, up a stairway, onto the stage, and then when they were on the stage, the ones who made eye contact with me earned a point. If they were smiling all the time, I'd give them another point. Then some of them would go to exit the stage on the right, and the smart ones made eye contact with me again one final time and smiled, and they got another point.

I was a judge. What was I supposed to do? What's the judging criteria? They don't tell you. But when the contestants were exiting the stage, if they would just pause and give me one last smile and one last piece of eye contact, they'd get another point.

That's why, when you play The Speaking Game, you earn a point just for smiling. It's so easy! But you have to think about it, and you have to do it. You <u>can</u> do it!

"Surf Lady" Veronica Grey is the best at smiling, and the best time to be smiling is when you're listening. When you're on TV and the host is talking to you, listen with a smile! It makes you look more likable.

Curtain calls for *The Magic Flute*, Royal Opera House, London

SING

Even If You
Can't Sing!

NOW, my dear reader, my dear friend, comes a very powerful part of The Speaking Game... It's called singing. When you're speaking, you can just *sing* anything!

I could sing anything I want, and it doesn't really matter what the tone is. Just sing because you feel like singing, and it changes the presentation and it's production value. And you get a full point! Put some singing in your presentation. Don't sing a song; just sing the words of your presentation. *Instead of talking, you can be singing!*

The more you do it, the easier it gets for you to really go for it. As you start doing all this stuff it's awkward. But the more you do it, the less awkward it becomes, and the more you can do anything with your voice.

Even if you're a bad singer, it doesn't matter. Lisa Sasevich sings when she's trying to "close" people into her $24,000 mastermind. It's amazing how she'll be in the closing portion of her sales pitch, and then she'll start singing a song about "shining bright like a diamond." That's her theme song, "Shine bright like a diamond"— and she's NOT a great singer.

Which makes it even better! — because it shows the audience that she's vulnerable, that she's not perfect, and it makes them believe that they don't have to be perfect. It shows that she's got flaws, that she's not a superstar. She's a real person. That's the point! When you're a bad singer and you can't sing great, it's even better when you dare to sing! It helps her make more money because she's willing to sing on stage. It's endearing. And I'll tell you, it's entertaining, which is the most important thing.

RHYMING

And now we get to the superstar stuff – rhyming. If you really want to be a great speaker, rhyme!

I went on YouTube and studied videos of "inspirational speakers who got a standing ovation." That's the search term I put in. I analyzed those videos — many, many, many of them ended with a rhyme.

Why do you think rappers are so exalted in their communities? Because they're rhyming!

Not everybody can rhyme. Rhyming is a sign of *superior* intelligence because most people don't rhyme. Didn't Jesus speak in verse? Didn't he rhyme a lot of messages? Look at his impact on the world. If you want to truly be a great speaker, or if you really want to engineer yourself to succeed with standing ovations as speaker, end with a rhyme.

I can't do it all the *time*,

But I know if you

get off your *dime*,

And say, "Heck! *I'm...*"

Willing to take *time*,

To memorize an actual *rhyme*,

People will think you're

sublime!

ACT-OUTS

ACT STUFF OUT!

THIS is an "act out" that I often do when I'm speaking on a stage:

> Where were you on December 31st, 1999? Were you at the ATM getting your "Y2K Money?" Were you partying with family and friends?

pursuing the Hollywood Dream. Naturally, on New Year's Eve of the Millennium, I was driving a taxi all around Los Angeles. That night there were two guys in the back seat of my cab who worked at Goldman Sachs.

"Did you hear about Mr. Carrera?" one asked the other. "He was the last guy they made Partner before the IPO, and in the IPO he cashed out a hundred million dollars!"

I turned around with a look of skepticism on my face: "Are you guys talking about Chris Carrera?"

Total shock in my back seat: "How do you know Mr. Carrera?"

Chris Carrera was a pledge in my fraternity at Wharton when I was pledge master. I used to make that little punk dance around the living room with his underpants on top of his head, and now *he* just scored a hundred million dollars as a partner at Goldman Sachs, and *I'm* driving a cab!

That night when it was all over I went home to my little boat in Marina Del Rey, and I climbed into my bunk wearing all my clothes, because it was the middle of winter and it was freezing. I pulled my down comforter around my body, and my wad of cash out of my sock, where I would hide my money when I was driving a cab so I wouldn't get robbed.

"Chris Carrera. Where was Chris Carrera tonight? The Rainbow Room? Man —I made five hundred and thirteen dollars driving a cab on New Year's Eve of the Millenium, and he's making a hundred million. It was not supposed to be this way!"

That's an act out.

Watch this act-out now at www.SpeakingGame.com

And when I do presentations like that — even at financial conferences — afterward, people in the audience come up to me to say, "That was the greatest sales presentation I've ever seen!" It's not a sales presentation. It's a one man show.

Act out stuff!

Act the whole thing out!

Donald Trump does it all the time. In every speech, he does an act out. He'll say something like:

> I was down at the World Trade Center, and I was talking to a construction worker I know, and the guy says, "Mr. Trump, are you going to build that wall?"
> I said, "Don't worry Joe! We're going to build the wall!"

He doesn't just *say* the words — He does an act out. He acts out the scene. He re-enacts what happened, playing all the parts himself.

He could've said, "I was down at the World Trade Center and one of the construction men asked me if we're going to build the wall. I assured him, we will build the wall."

You can see the difference. They're the same exact thing, except one is showbiz, and the other is **boring.**

You've got to put in act-outs because *when you're a speaker*

you're an entertainer.

EXTERNALIZE

YOUR *INTERNAL*

MONOLOGUE

This is a super powerful technique: giving voice to your private thoughts in your mind. I learned this from another one of my many mentors, Sean Stephenson, "The 3-foot giant." He was born with a bone disease, so he's only three feet tall and rides around in a wheelchair all the time — and he's one of the best speakers in the world. Think about that: 3' tall, confined to a wheel chair, world-class speaker. Incredible! And this is his main *shtick*. This is exactly what he does. (I know, because I went to his seminar three times.)

The first time I saw him, he had his assistants carry him onto the stage in his wheelchair, then they dumped him out of the wheelchair onto the ground, then they turned out all the lights, and then you hear Sean Stephenson:

"August twenty second, two thirty-seven a.m. Huh? What? Where am I? What happened? I'm on the floor. Oh no! Oh no! My arm is broken! I broke my arm again! Why is this happening to me? Again! Again! A broken arm — I can't have this happen to me! Next month a hundred and fifty people are coming to my seminar! Why is this happening to me?? — Why?!?!"

That's his whole shtick. He does that all the time. *He externalizes his internal monologue*. You hear what he's thinking. It's a trick. He lets the audience *into his mind!*

Now when I was doing my act-out a few pages back, about being on the boat, that's exactly what I was doing. I was externalizing my internal monologue. I wasn't in the boat saying those things. I was in my bunk *thinking* those things. But to make it entertaining for the audience, I can't just *think* — I have to *speak*, because you can't read my mind. However, the audience is smart enough to know that something is going on and it's got truth to it. That's what this is all about— displaying some kind of truth about what's going on in your mind.

It took me five years of maniacal pursuit of success as a speaker, going to seminar after seminar — I went to 30-40 seminars a year for five years, studying hundreds of speakers, before I discovered and started implementing this.

And when you start implementing the externalization of your internal monologue into your act out, do you get a point for that? Yes, you get a point for an act out, and an **extra** point for the externalization of your internal monologue! What a great way to win points in The Speaking Game — Super advanced!

MORE WAYS TO SCORE POINTS!

Use your tongue. There's lots of ways. Stick it out. Stick it in your cheek. Run it over your lips or teeth. Be creative. Provocative. Use your imagination!

Use a prop. Anything you hold in your hands is a prop. Cars are props. So are animals. And kids. Props transform a flat talking head performance into something 3-dimensional.

Use your lips. Chris Rock does a whole heck of a lot with his lips. Lots of fertile ground here.

Nostrils. *Flares. Sniffs. Wow!*

Clint & Chris Rock

Involve your feet. This is very advanced performance technique. Dance, use your shoes as props, tap your foot, be creative — but only if you're ready to really be bold!

Use your Ears. Tug. Cup. Pull. Holy cow!

Foreign Language — another very advanced technique is to use foreign words or expressions in your performance.

On *Iron Chef America* I complimented Iron Chef Kat Cora's dish as being *"Magnifique!"*

In stage performances I always try to include one simple Spanish word.

Foreign language makes you much more interesting.

HOW TO CREATE & PERFECT A SPEECH

Speech Creation

If you're a speaker, the way to create a speech is to say what you want to say. That is not, of course, going to be the final draft of the speech. It's just a *first draft*.

Say what you want to say on audio. Create the speech.

If you can't do it all in one shot, a lot of times what I'll do is open up a voice memo recording app on my iPhone and record as much as I can think of at the moment. Then I'll press Pause, and think *what do I want to say next?* Then I'll record that. And then I'll press pause, and think some more. Then I'll record some more and keep going like this until I run out of things to say. Then I'll press Pause again. You just keep going until you've created your speech, for however long you want to speak. If it's a five-minute speech you do it for five minutes. If it's a 10-minute speech you do it for 10 minutes. Just keep adding more ideas and more words, and record it all until you've created your speech.

Once you've created your speech, either type it up yourself or send it to a transcription service and have them transcribe it. Check the transcription. You don't want any mistakes that could throw you off.

Now you have a printout of what you actually said.

Now you can see how many times "umms" and "ahs" are in your speech, accidentally. Those words are not good. Read your speech. You'll find all the things that you don't want in your speech. Edit them out.

So, you create the speech, transcribe it, edit it, and once you've got it edited into the final format, you could say that, ideally, this is exactly what you want to say.

NOW LET'S talk about rehearsing and how to rehearse. I already mentioned that a huge aspect of Donald Trump's success is that he rehearses so much. Let's add some specifics to that.

Write It Out by Hand

Once you've created your whole "ideal" speech, it's time to memorize it. The best way to memorize it is to *write it out by hand*. I know it's hard work, and it takes a lot of time, and it may hurt your hand to do it — especially if it's a long speech — but if you write it out by hand, you're making it physical. You will see the words with your eyes as they come out of your fingers. This impresses the words into your mind in multiple dimensions and multiple modalities. It helps you to memorize. Now you're going to memorize it…

Beyond Memorization!

Memorizing your speech is good, but it's not enough. You need to memorize your speech **beyond memorization.** If you have to think *What am I supposed to say next?* that's **weak.** I'm never in front of an audience thinking *What am I supposed to say next?* I'm just up there talking — because I know my topic. You've got to <u>know</u> your speech. Cold.

I hate presenters who rely on their slides. I'm not going to mention names, but I once paid $9,500 to go to a seminar with a presenter who had the nerve to just show his slides and read the words on the slides. That's all he did. Can you believe that? He expected 18 CEO's to sit there for what was supposed to be to a three-day seminar, while he just read the words directly off his slides. (And by the way, the seminar ended at 1:00PM on day 3 — I don't call it a three-day seminar when it ends at 1:00pm on day 3 — that's a 2+ day seminar!)

You've got to know your material, and you have to know it beyond memorization. You have to have true expertise and command of your subject matter.

That happens from memorization and the iteration that comes out of all of the rehearsal you've done. Then you're going to start speaking your speech after you've memorized it. **Speak the speech <u>out loud</u>** as part of your memorization process.

Once you can speak the whole speech, or even if you can only speak the whole speech in portions — perhaps you will learn the first five minutes, then the next five minutes —then you record it onto a loop and play it over and over all night long while you sleep.

Voice Loop

Record your speech on a loop and play it all night long while you sleep. (It's a 99¢ APP) Why play it while you sleep? So, it sinks into your subconscious mind.

Dan Kennedy taught me this technique. Dan was the longest running speaker in the entire Peter Lowe *Success Seminars* circuit, appearing on the same stage in the same arenas as George Bush, Colin Powell and Donald Trump. He gave his "Magnetic Marketing" speech, and sold more "stuff" at those events than any other speaker. He's made millions of dollars with that speech, and he told me he would play that speech on a loop, over and over and over. And he'd say that speech the same way, every time, comma for comma, and pause for pause. It was always the same, because when you have a winning speech you don't change the speech, you change your audience.

The loop is a super-powerful technique in rehearsal.

Once you've got your speech on a loop, and you can speak it, then it's about performance. Every performance you do is a rehearsal for the next performance. I've done VIP Speaker Training 15 times, and every time I enjoy it because it's a rehearsal for the next time. And I always set them up right before *Celebrity Launchpad,* so I can use the training as a rehearsal and warmup for my 4-day celebrity transformation event.

PERFORMANCE

IS

REHEARSAL

"People don't like to rehearse, because you suck when you rehearse, but if you don't suck when you rehearse you will suck when you perform."

-Michael Port

PROFESSIONAL SPEAKERS
PROCESS

1. Speak/Create

2. Transcribe

3. Read

4. Edit

5. Write Out by Hand

6. Memorize

7. Speak

8. Loop

9. Perform

SPEAKER MARKETING

Being a
7-Figure Speaker
is really about is about
making
SOMETHING
out of
NOTHING

THE ENTIRE TRICK TO BEING A
7-FIGURE SPEAKER IS TO
"MAKE SOMETHING OUT OF NOTHING"

When we come into this world we're nothing. We're just a blubbering blob — a person, just like every other person in the world.

Our goal as VIP speakers is to create something out of that nothingness. In the way we position ourselves with our credibility, and in the way we speak — to make something out of nothing.

A person who is an award-winning speaker should be a good speaker. So, if you are an award-winning speaker, feature it in your bio. If you're not an award-winning speaker you should try to become an award-winning speaker, or at least a frequent speaker.

IF YOU'RE NOT AN AWARD-WINNING SPEAKER, YOUR BIO SHOULD AT LEAST SAY THAT YOU'RE A <u>FREQUENT SPEAKER</u> ON YOUR TOPIC.

ECTION ALERT

Clint Arthur
LEADERSHIP & PERFORMANCE EXPERT

f 🐦 @FOXBUSINESS

WHEN you are a speaker there will be a photo of you in a program, or in some publication that describes who the speakers are. Your positioning and credibility work begins with that "Marketing" piece.

One of the most powerful ways to position yourself as someone special is by using a photo of you from the media. That gives you a third-party endorsement as somebody special.

Very often, my head shot will be a photograph of me taken as a screen shot from a media appearance.

You should also feature awards that you have won — because very few people actually win awards.

THE IMPORTANCE OF YOUR PHOTO

I took a frame out of my TV appearance on *Mornings with Maria* and use it as part of my email signature, but not just the frame itself — I superimposed an award medallion I created to represent my *Record Sales achievement*. I want people to know that Celebrity is about making money!

When you win awards, create graphic images to represent the award so you can use it for your marketing.

A GREAT HEADSHOT

IS ABOUT YOUR HEAD

Never underestimate the power and importance of a great headshot.

Very often, *your headshot is the very first piece of marketing* **a prospect will see.**

Invest time and money **in getting a** *collection* **of great** *headshots* **you can use in a variety of circumstances.**

Great *headshots make you money!*

Speaker photos that do not include audience are missing the entire point of being a VIP Speaker.

You speak in front of audiences to demonstrate that lots of people think you are a very smart person, and that by listening to you, their lives will be improved and/or they will make more money.

You gotta have audience IN THE PHOTOS!

That's why *Business Expert Forum at Harvard Faculty Club* guarantees my clients great video & photos with audience.

TESTIMONIALS

You absolutely MUST have testimonials on your speaker page or website, raving about what a great speaker you are and what great information you deliver.
If you don't have them, you are kidding yourself about your ability to make the impact you want to make, the influence you want to have, and the income you desire.

Ron Douglas: "I Highly Recommend You Book Clint Arthur as a Speaker"

Clint Arthur • 13 views • 5 months ago

http://www.ClintArthur.TV #CelebritySalesSecrets

Ron Douglas: "Clint's keynote rocked the Warrior Event"

Clint Arthur • 6 views • 1 year ago

http://www.ClintArthur.TV

Pick a phrase from the person's testimonial to use as the title of the video on YouTube.

Include "context" in the video if it enhances the status of the video or adds visual interest.

VIDEOS OF YOUR SPEECH

"LIFE BEGINS WHERE YOUR COMFORT ZONE ENDS"

CLINT ARTHUR

3-camera • HD • Professionally Edited

Clint Arthur interviews the actor who portrays
"The Most Interesting Man In The World"
in Dos Equis beer advertisements

Clint Arthur with mentor Brendon Burchard

Sexy Talk Titles

If you want to get paid for speeches you need a very sexy talk tile, and a powerful 1-sheet to sell it. Here's mine:

CELEBRITY SALES SECRETS

The 9 Strategies Superstars Use to Increase Impact, Influence, Income... And How YOU Can Too!

Personal Stories, Videos and Interactive Exercises facilitate a Fun, Exciting and Entertaining Transformational Experience

Clooney

Elvis

Lady Gaga

"Entertainers-In-Chief"

Beatles

Robert Downey Jr.

Isaac Mizrahi

Trump

You

Clint Arthur   *www.ClintArthur.TV*   **310-415-0450**

Travolta

EVERYBODY KNOWS, CELEBRITIES.

Simon

Robin

Ringo

Snookie

Hoda

122

Trump

..HANG OUT WITH CELEBRITIES

planethollyw

Brooke

Snoop

Jane Lynch, "Glee"

"41"

Your

"Speaker Introduction"

Should be short and powerful.

Needs to position you as somebody worth listening to.

Less is always more.

If you can, use your sizzle reel to do the heavy lifting of your intro, because ***most people who introduce you will do a lousy job....***

Here's my sizzle reel: www.is.gd/ClintSizzle

CLINT ARTHUR
BIO/SPEAKER INTRODUCTION

CLINT ARTHUR is the #1 Bestselling author of
What They Teach You at The Wharton Business School
and
Break Through Your Upper Limits on TV

Clint's "Mathematical Formula for Getting on TV anytime you want for FREE" has transformed 648+ Authors, Speakers, Coaches & Entrepreneurs into **Celebrities** who booked themselves on more than 3524 Network TV appearances with ABC NBC CBS FOX News & Talk Shows that he's aware of *SO FAR*.

Clint has also arranged for MORE THAN 300 clients to speak at Harvard, West Point, NASDAQ, Coca-Cola and Microsoft.

Dan Kennedy anointed Clint his *Info-Marketer of The Year,* and calls him "The Real Thing"

Lisa Sasevich calls Clint her "Secret Weapon"

You will call him your "New Be-Eff-Eff"

Please welcome, CLINT ARTHUR!

FREEDOM

I used to think that being a rock-n-roll singer was the ultimate freedom.

Today I know that being a Celebrity Speaker is the best "profession" in the world. All you have to do is show up and talk, then people give you lots of money. What could possibly be better than that?

I put the word "profession" in quotes because the Speaking part is hardly even work at all — it's fun!

SPEAKERS WITH GAME

In My Humble Opinion, these are the best speakers & mentors I've had the privilege to study, either in person or on video, and who have been most influential to me in my career as a speaker. Treat this section like a bible of the important things you need to learn from speakers for your further study. Speaking requires you to study other speakers! Everything you need to learn about speaking is contained in the lives and live performances of the following people:

DAN KENNEDY

has had the greatest influence on me of anyone I have ever studied with, including all of my professors at Wharton or Stuyvesant High School.

Dan is a marketing genius and one of the most interesting success stories ever to come out of the world of public speaking. His primary philosophy is "No-BS" and that is a great way to describe his style, which is the opposite of flash, the opposite of slick, the opposite of everything everyone else is doing, purposely and by express design.

Dan led me down the golden path of *manufacturing* celebrity for my personal brand, and as this has been so much fun, it has become my primary focus and obsession for all my marketing. While many people find him to be gruff, **Ali and I love him like a father and appreciate his brilliance and genuine loyalty and kindheartedness towards animals and people he cares about,** and we feel privileged to consider ourselves among the latter.

His protégés include many of the biggest names in the experts industry, including many of the names in this bibliography of speakers; James Malinchak, Mike Koenigs, Frank Kern, Russell Brunson, Robin Robins, Joe Polish and many others too numerable to list. He is known as "The Millionaire Maker" for very good reason, and I give him my highest endorsement and greatest indebted appreciation for the impact on my life.

LISA SASEVICH: "The Queen of Sales Conversion" has been one of my greatest mentors and friends in the experts industry. She has several uncanny abilities:

1) **She is The Most Likable Person In The World.** You want her to like you, and you want to be her friend. She is just so freaking likable it's amazing!

Clint, Lisa, Juan, Ali

2) She makes you understand that if you are selling something that truly helps people and you let them get away without buying from you, you are actually doing them a huge disservice. (What a powerful skill that is!!!!)

She has taught me some invaluable things:

1) **Transformation occurs at the moment of transaction.** As soon as a person gives you money, that's a sign that they've actually committed, and as a result, they instantly achieve a transformation!

2) **Be the client you want to attract.** This is so incredibly powerful!

3) **It doesn't have to be perfect.** The first time I made 6 figures selling from the stage it was at her *Speak to Sell Bootcamp* — and it was far from perfect!

Check out Lisa at **www.TheInvisibleClose.com**

JAMES MALINCHAK

"The Big-Money Speaker" is the man who opened my eyes to 2 major aspects of my success:

At a mastermind in his home, James said: "What Clint is doing with Local TV is genius because it's right out of *The 21 Immutable Laws of Marketing*. He's not the first person in PR or Publicity, he's not the first person in TV PR and Publicity, but he is the first and only person in Local TV PR and Publicity. You must be first in a category. If you can't be first in a category then you must put one foot outside the category to make a new sub-category, which is what Clint has done with Local TV Publicity and PR — which is why what he's doing is so genius."

James also opened my eyes to the magical powers of Celebrity Attachment. I attended an immensely valuable workshop at his house on just this topic alone, and since that day my career has never been the same — it's been a rocket ride!

If you are looking for training on how to make money as a college speaker, that is James' unique positioning in the speaker training world — he teaches you how to make big money speaking on the college circuit, and he's the only one who does it. www.BigMoneySpeaker.com

JONATHAN SPRINKLES: "Your Connection Coach"

is a phenomenal performer and speaker, and a tremendous speaker coach. My mom and I were both Platinum coaching clients with Jonathan, and he is single-handedly responsible for making me feel like I was entitled to use my personal story. This was huge! He also taught me about and got me started with act-outs. www.JSprinkles.com

MIKE KOENIGS:

One of the very nicest and most sincere people I know in the Experts Industry, Mike is one of the rare people who also guarantees results for his seminar attendees. He is a true expert on how to Publish & Profit, and how to seemingly Be Everywhere Now in the eyes of your customers and prospects. I am most indebted to Mike for his genuine friendship, guidance, and for being a living example of how to be a nice guy and a powerful sales person at the same time. He is generous in everything he does, and always gives genuine heartfelt advise — the kind of advice he'd want someone to give him. www.YouEverywhereNow.com

DONALD TRUMP — Regardless of how you may feel about him politically, you cannot ignore his success as a speaker, earning $1 million per appearance for years, and having spoken in so many arena performances over the course of his decades long career as a public speaker. I studied and wrote about him in my previous book "21 Performance Secrets of Donald Trump," and my wife, Ali, says it is probably the best thing I've ever written.

ROGER LOVE — The supreme "voice" teacher working today, with deep and advanced knowledge about the needs and

special circumstances pertaining to speakers (as opposed to singers). Roger's impressive list of celebrity clients including Tony Robbins and Suze Orman positions him as "Hollywood's Go-To Guy" and as a justifiably high-priced coach and consultant, so if he accepts you as a client you can expect it to come at a rather significant investment — but the best is always expensive. Please let him know Clint sent you.

GRANT CARDONE:

The Top Sales Expert and trainer working in the world today, Grant is a powerhouse of content creation with his many homemade, self distributed TV shows and videos that he posts into his social media feeds at an astounding rate.

I have been most impressed and most influenced by his performance as an audio book creator, giving voice to his latest bestseller, *"Be Obsessed or Be Average."* His philosophy is extreme, but his performance as the sole voice of that book was incredible!

If you want to learn about sales, GrantCardone.com is a fantastic place to invest some time and money. And if you want to learn about performing stories with high energy and personal charisma, start watching Grant's endless video streams.

ROY H. WILLIAMS: The author of multiple best-selling books in his *"Wizard of Ads"* series, Roy is a super intelligent deep thinker on the subject of advertising, direct response, and character as it relates to personal branding and corporate image. I have had the pleasure of seeing Roy speak several times at his Wizards Academy, and he always gives an enlightening, entertaining, and inspirational entrepreneurial presentation. I also am a regular listener to his Monday Morning Memo podcast, which I honestly believe EVERYONE should subscribe to at www.MondayMorningMemo.com

133

JOEL OSTEEN is my FAVORITE speaker of all time. I listen to his message of HOPE and FAITH in a BETTER WORLD any time I need an extra "something" in my day, any time I want to feel like the world is a better place, a safer place, a richer place, a happier place, or a place I truly belong. I started out as a fan of his writing when I read his book *It's Your Time*.

Then I was blessed to discover his podcast, and it is my go-to resource for something GOOD to listen to while I'm on my daily walks. This man is a GIFT to humanity, and one of the most joyous lights in my life.

ALEX MANDOSSIAN is a very smart man who rose to prominence in the world of Internet Marketing through his deep knowledge of funnels, and more recently with his work on live webinars. He is a deep thinker and always gets your brain going with provocative ideas and a very clean and powerful stage presentation if you have the privilege to see him speak in person. Alex was my number one referrer and affiliate for Business Expert Forum at Harvard Faculty Club in 2015, and when he attended *Celebrity Launchpad* he actually paid me $500 over full price because he thought the value was so much more than what I was asking as an investment, and he wanted me to tell this story every single time I speak about him, as I've just done (again!)

TRACY REPCHUK is one of the smartest female speakers I have ever seen or had the pleasure to work with. When Tracy attended *Celebrity Launchpad* she spent zero time chitchatting, and spent the entire time working on individual proposals for individual producers, resulting in her getting booked on 13 of the 15 TV show opportunities, including on ABC Chicago, with a proposal on social media safety for kids. She speaks all over the world, and is a real pro when it comes to presenting and selling from stage.

DEAN GRAZIOSI is someone you have seen countless times on infomercials in the middle of the night, selling his real estate investing courses direct to camera with a super likable, super trustworthy, boy next-door personality that is irresistible. He is one of the smartest thinkers I met during my two year membership in Genius Network, and a magnificent presenter both on stage and on camera. He really understands how to be natural when he speaks, and after so many years of continuous presence on television, he is a genius at delivering sales messages direct to camera.

DANIEL WHITTINGTON, Vice-Chancellor of Wizards Academy, is an immensely talented performer and presenter, with a diverse skill-set and knowledge base which he draws upon with tireless energy and limitless passion for entrepreneurs who come to the fabulous campus and learning environment he

curates and leads in the outskirts of Austin, TX. Ali and I have been and continue to be magically attracted into his unique presence and domain despite the fact that his main passion and impact these days seems to be his phenomenal *Whiskey Vault* podcast — and I don't even drink alcohol any more! Daniel's vast knowledge and entertainment value are powerful attractors into his unique educational environment.

SUSAN BRATTON is a brilliant and beautiful magnum of passion and contagious energy for her topic of supercharged sexual connection and better relationships. Out of all my students ever to come through *Celebrity Launchpad,* Susan has taken to and embraced the concept of costume more powerfully and effectively than anyone I've ever had the privilege to work with. Her marathon live streams and live webinars are worth every second of your time and attention, if only to soak up her seductive personal power and energy, and to appreciate her many costume changes which will entertain and titillate you. It's almost unfair that she has all the assets that she does, but that's good for you and me as members of her lucky audience!

SURIA SPARKS

is the top social media influencer in Singapore, and leads a very passionate tribe of followers and downline participants, many of whom start with her in poverty and progress rapidly with her to enormous prosperity. As a speaker she has appeared with some of the biggest names speaking on stages today, including Sir Richard Branson and Gary Vaynerchuk, and as a teacher she has delivered some of the most impressive speakers I have ever seen to participate in *Business Expert Forum at Harvard Faculty Club.*

BOB PROCTOR is a living legend in the speaking industry, and justifiably so. He has an enormous personal presence and a deep knowledge of how to move and motivate people based on his decades of experience as a professional speaker. You have seen him in the movie "The Secret," but if you have

never seen him speak in person you have missed a great opportunity to witness the power of a man who knows how to communicate effectively. I have been particularly impressed by his vocal power and abilities to maintain and audience's attention through vocal volume modulation and punctuation. Definitely an impressive influence in my performance techniques.

JORGE CRUISE is a genius in terms of understanding how to stay relevant and maintain presence in the media through consistent releases of best-selling books. Working in the

most competitive genre of all, weight loss, this man has maintained a constant presence on the biggest television shows over nearly 2 decades, and it is truly worth your time and attention to investigate what he does and how he does it if you have any aspirations of making a name for yourself in media. He will also help you lose a few pounds and tighten up your belly!

TIM FERRISS is a multiple New York Times best-selling author, and if you are in his target market he will appear to be everywhere you look when he is releasing a new book. Then, once you are alerted to him, he will be in your life forever with his amazing podcast and seemingly never-ending and broadening media presence. Tim Ferriss is positioned as one of the smartest people in the world when it comes to improving your life, and he very well may actually be the genius that he seems to be. I listen to his podcast all the time because I always feel like it will make me smarter and better.

VERONICA GREY was my very first local TV publicity protégé, booking herself on 10 television shows within just a few weeks of enrolling in my training. She has since gone on to become the most televised female surfer of all time, and now counts Leonardo DiCaprio, Justin Bieber, and the worlds top pro surfer John John Florence as her best homies. Veronica is a unique force of nature as an environmental activist, shark safety advocate, and was recognized as Supermodel of the Decade by *Business Expert Forum at Harvard Faculty Club.*

TRACY HERBERT has undergone one of the most incredible transformations ever produced by Celebrity Launchpad and Business Expert Forum at Harvard Faculty Club. My wife, Ali, discovered Tracey at a conference several years ago and after hearing her story about surviving type one diabetes 20 years passed her

original life expectancy, was able to convince her to come into our world and share her amazing message, spirit, and passion for life with an ever growing community of diabetics. Today Tracy is a very active and nationally recognized paid speaker and media personality who recently appeared on Dr. Oz as combination of her trans continental bicycle journey to promote diabetes awareness. If you have diabetes and want coaching on how to survive and thrive with your disease, you should run and embrace whatever she offers.

JOEL WELDON: one of the nicest people you will ever meet, Joel has been taking home 7-figures a year as a motivational speaker for decades. He is also a phenomenal speaker coach with his Ultimate Speaker System and community, of which I am a member. Joel has a unique ability to coach speakers and make you feel great about the criticism he gives, all of which is right on the money. Joel has been making big money as a fee-based speaker for so long that when I told him I make money by paying to speak, he had to do a special interview on the topic for his Ultimate Speaker community. www.SuccessComesInCans.com

SEAN STEPHENSON:

"The 3-Foot Giant" is a true force of nature wrapped up in an adorable and physically precarious package! He is always one of the very best speakers at any event he graces with his presence, and I have learned so much about the craft of being a great

performer as a result of my multiple attendances at his *10K Speeches* seminar. His teachings and example are responsible for me progressing to any levels of professional subtlety that I may have accomplished, and I'm most grateful and indebted to him. www.SeanStephenson.com

DAVID BACH:

I met David at *Experts Academy* in 2010, and his words to me that day changed my life forever, shaping my entire perspective on commitment to TV and being a celebrity.

David Bach told me:

"I've been on every TV show in America, and as a result, when I got my big break to be on the Oprah Winfrey Show, I was able to hit it out of the park because I knew how to press the audience's buttons, I knew how to work with props and have talking points that were great for TV. As a result of that I became a repeat guest on Oprah, a regular guest on the Today Show with over 100 appearances, and had 11 New York Times Bestselling books which sold more than 11,000,000 copies of the ...*Finish Rich* series.

David Bach has been a true inspiration to me, and has provided millions of people with guidance to help them Finish Rich! www.DavidBach.com

Dr. KELLYANN PETRUCCI is one of the most driven and passionate doctors I have ever met in my life. Her knowledge of nutrition and health is deep and sincere, but it is her drive that has taken her to the tremendous prominence she has achieved in life. After attending *Celebrity Launchpad* twice, you have doubtless seen Kellyann on her multiple hits with Good

Morning America, and regularly on Dr. Oz. Two of her books have justifiably risen to the exalted status of *New York Times* bestseller's on the topic of Bone Broth.

VANESSA HORN

is one of the most successful female coaches in the MLM world, speaking on giant stages in arenas. After attending *Celebrity Launchpad*, she proved that you can get every single one of your appearances confirmed and shot if you want it bad enough and are

doggedly determined enough to make it happen. She is a lovely person, a beautiful woman, and a great coach.

ANGELA WILLIAMS

is a woman with a powerful mission to a eradicate child sexual abuse. Her Voice Today movement took her from *Celebrity Launchpad* all the way to CNN International in front of 360 million households in less than two months because she is so driven and passionate about making a difference in the lives of so many innocents.

HAL ELROD

came to me already a great speaker with a great story and a great book — but a book that nobody had ever bought yet. We had to make a special payment plan for him so that he could afford to come to *Celebrity Launchpad,* and come he did! Hal got booked by almost every producer, and as you can see in his case study on www.guaranteedcelebrity.com he has been using these evergreen marketing videos to fuel the engine of his self publishing phenomenon, *The Miracle Morning,* which has already sold more than 90,000 copies without a major publisher or distributor, all on his own. Hal is an amazingly energetic and inspirational speaker and well worth studying. *The Miracle Morning* has changed many people lives, and very likely will change yours if you go for it.

TOM CHENAULT and I met at his inauguration into the Multi Level Marketing Hall of Fame, more than five years ago. Since then I have watched him *blow up* his new MLM company, and have had the privilege to appear on his radio show in Colorado several times. I always enjoy watching his

live streams on Facebook and appreciate his commitment to sobriety and his empowerment of the people in his organization. If you are looking for an inspirational speaker and leader who can help you generate a fantastic income running your own business with his proven process, don't hesitate to investigate www.tomchenault.com

DAVE DEE was at one time Dan Kennedy's most visible protégé, as chief marketing officer of GKIC and co-star of the *New Magnetic Marketing* product Dan produced a few years ago. Dave has become a highly influential mentor of mine through his *Psychic Salesman* trainings which I wisely invested in, and his *Million-dollar Presentation Workshop* which I also had the great wisdom to invest in and attend. Dave has his roots in the world of stage magic, and as such is a seasoned and practiced showman in addition to being an expert at sales and business presentations. He is also a fine gentleman and a brilliant marketing mind who has had a profound impact on me and my career in selling from stage.

RYAN DEISS runs one of the largest, most successful Internet Marketing conferences in the world, *Traffic & Conversion Summit*, at which I will be exhibiting as a high-level sponsor for my fourth time in 2018. He is so youthful and boyishly good looking that it's hard to believe he is running such a mega-successful multi-million dollar marketing and event company, and it is worth studying his low-key stage style by sheer virtue of the fact that it works so well and seems so unstudied, un-produced, and unrehearsed. Attending T&C is something everyone should do, if only to see what is currently the cutting edge of Internet Marketing. Warning: you will want to pull out your credit card and invest in lots of really great stuff at this event, which would be a smart move for anyone who will actually implement.

JEFF WALKER was on the main stage at Experts Academy the first time I attended, back in 2010, and was already something of a living legend in the industry by virtue of the fact that he invented the *Product Launch Formula* everyone was using to

make oodles and boodles of cash with their internet product launches.

The first time I saw Jeff on stage he was wearing a gray flannel suit and was playing with the change or keys in his pants pockets the whole time he spoke, so I thought to myself: *if Jeff Walker can keep his hands in his pockets the whole time he's on stage, I can do that too!* This resulted in a hugely horrible habit that required me to physically safety-pin my pockets closed in order to break myself free of this faux-pas hand position. Since then Jeff has really evolved in his performance, developing quite the "aw shucks" and "super nice guy" low-key persona on stage that makes you feel like you want to be his friend and that he is one of the most likable people in the world, which I'm sure he probably really is. A brilliant marketing mind worth studying and learning from at one of his PLF live events.

RUSSELL BRUNSON is another Dan Kennedy protégé, having won *Marketer of the Year*, and having appeared on the main stage at GKIC events many many times. Russell has a very low-key persona, embodying his Idaho lifestyle and unlikely Internet millionaire storyline. He has created an empire of Click Funnels and other Internet marketing master tools that are making millions and millions of dollars for him, and even more money for his customers. You cannot argue with the success of this boy next-door turned marketing titan, and as a speaker he is another one of the very natural and unassuming style of stage presenters who makes tons and tons of money selling from the stage.

ROBIN ROBINS is another Dan Kennedy protégé who runs marketing Boot Camps for the information technology industry that would do uncle Dan very proud. Her events are like the Dan Kennedy events I remember when I first got involved going to his Super-Conference back in 2011. Giant audiences, properly entertained and educated with excellent marketing at lavish and expertly produced big time events staged in gigantic hotel ball rooms in a very first class way. Robin Robins is the real deal and probably the most successful female event host and promoter I know in the marketing world. If you are a woman you would be well advised to study her methodologies and performance style by sheer virtue of her tremendous success. If you are in the IT space you need to learn what she is teaching. If you are any kind of speaker who wants to sell more from the stage, she is a proven formula of success worth emulating.

SALLY HOGSHEAD is a best-selling author and phenomenal speaker. I really do mean phenomenal! The 10 minute talk she gave about her son Asher at the 2016 Genius Network meeting was the smartest and best stage presentation I've ever seen, and truly embodied her main philosophy which is *to Fascinate*. I am hard-pressed to think of anyone who is her equal as a speaker on stage. Her artfulness makes it hard to study from her though because she makes it look so seamless and easy that it's really difficult to see what she's actually "doing." (Is she actually doing anything? Or is she just a natural? I really don't know because she is that good!)

MARIA BARTIROMO has had a long career on television and currently hosts one of the very best business news programs on TV, *"Mornings with Maria"* — and although I have had the privilege to be on the show twice, neither one of those appearances were on days

when she was actually there. She has been On-Air talent for so long that she is seemingly completely natural in the way that she delivers brilliant questions and interacts so intelligently with the highest level business and political guests including top CEOs and Government leaders. She happens to be married to one of my fraternity brothers who is a complete and total genius, so I know that her IQ is real and she is as insightful as she really seems. If you are a woman or a man who wants to be great on television, you must watch Maria and see what true television performance excellence really looks like day after day. Oh — and on top of all that, she is a total babe!

DAGEN McDOWELL has been the host on FOX Business Network both times I had the privilege to appear on their "air," and she is a very gracious and professional broadcaster who knows how to make a guest look good! She has a charming combination of Southern charm and Wall Street no-nonsense manners, which makes her fascinating and alluring, even beyond her beauty — which is considerable.

LEE CARTER has been sitting across from me at the other end of the desk on both of my appearances for "Mornings with Maria" and has impressed me to no end. This is one smart and skillful television personality and performer, with amazingly gorgeous teeth and hair, and a sharp quick witted mind that is ready to talk about any topic under the sun. I wish she would take me under her wing and be my mentor!

Seriously. She runs a Communications firm in New York City with major corporate clients and really knows how to play the Celebrity-TV-Business trifecta to the max. What a superstar!

WITH HODA KOTB

HODA KOTB has the most beautiful teeth I've ever seen. She is a lovely person whom I met in studio when I went to coach my client Sandi Masori on the today show, and when I got a selfie with Hoda I was so blown away by her teeth up close I was inspired to get Zoom teeth whitening the next week — and every day I still dream about having teeth as beautiful as hers — yes, every day of my life. She is a seasoned professional broadcaster and has ridden out a multi year tenure on *The Today Show*, and anyone who aspires to just be a natural and nice person on TV should study her performances every morning. Such an inspirational person!

MIKE TYSON shared some serious wisdom with me in Las Vegas: I asked him what was the most important thing he ever learned, and he said "Stay humble." Today Mike is working hard as a speaker on stage doing his one-man show night after night after night, and I have a lot of respect for what he has created for himself and how he is

using the stories of his life to create this next chapter of the Mike Tyson story. It's very interesting to study the way he has constructed his show and the way he is able to get up there and put it all together day after day considering the significant beating that his brain has undergone over his many years as a professional boxer.

JIM CRAMER delivers a fascinating blend of Wall Street trader and TV show-biz personality to his daily stock market show, *Mad Money* on CNBC. The man is an entertainer and his TV show uses every trick in the book and then some to keep what could be a dry topic very entertaining and moving along with tremendous energy. This accounts for his tremendous success and I use him as a teaching tool in my Celebrity Launchpad classes to demonstrate the power of props and demonstrations and Voice technique on television. Kramer is an inspiration for me because of my background at the Wharton business school and my passion for performing on TV and I am most indebted to his tremendous example of how to blend finance and showbiz day after day and continuously keep it interesting and fun.

FRANK CALIENDO is one of the few people who is video I show at Celebrity Launchpad who is still alive. Frank and bodies in the power of "how you say things being more important than what you actually say" and I use his coach John Madden impersonation on the David Letterman show as one of my favorite teaching tools. It's very tough to get people to understand that how you say what you say is way more important than what you actually say, and Frank Caliendo, to me, provides the ultimate example of this precept. He is a tremendously funny and talented entertainer and I really appreciate his skills more than he will ever know.

HOWARD STERN has been a tremendous inspiration to me over many decades, and well before I was ever thinking about being a professional speaker. When I was renovating my first cosmetic fixer house in the deep slums of the San Fernando Valley, every morning  when I drove to work I would listen to Howard Stern on the radio — it was the only fun I had all day long. Howard was my soul piece of joy every day for three months. He is the greatest example anyone could have about how important it is to be true to your own self and not listen to others, to follow your own internal guidance and only do what you believe to be authentic and true for you. Did Jeni win unique entertainer, Howard has in the course of his career dominated all media, and as a result, Become an inspiration to millions, and a talent well worth studying for clues of greatness.

TOM LEYKIS was the one thing that got me through the drudgery of being a taxi driver for six years. Every Friday night I would pick up my taxi from the dispatch yard, and turn on my pocket-size transistor radio and Jam it into the leather door pull of whichever shitty Crown Victoria they'd give me that week. And there would be

151

the Tom Leykis show, old faithful, on 97.1 talk radio. It was just what I needed, when I needed something most, something to get me through the bitter months and years post break-up with baby's mama, something to keep my spirits up and entertain me as I drove around earning the tens and 20s which allowed me to survive all those years chasing my Hollywood dream. I truly don't know what I would have done if I did not have *The Professor* entertain me for those first few hours of driving the cab on Friday nights. I'm so grateful to him — it's hard to believe. Just his voice was enough to keep me going all those many years. "Blow me up, Tom!"

KEVIN HARRINGTON was one of the original sharks on "Shark Tank," and is a tremendously entertaining performer and speaker on stages and on camera. I am most indebted to him for proving to me the value of having a .TV website, and it is because of him that I use www.ClintArthur.TV. I recently saw him speak at a mastermind, and gave him "Daily Zig" as an idea for how to exploit a Zig property he controls. Hope it helps spread the good works of Zig Ziglar!

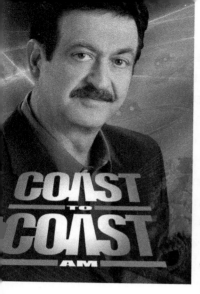

GEORGE NOORY is the brilliant host of "Coast to Coast AM with George Noory," one of the largest syndicated radio shows in the world, and the first show to give me a real break when I was starting out with The Last Year of Your Life program, before I even really consider myself speaker. I was just coach, and I had just had this tremendous experience of living as if I and the rest of the men on my team we're going to die at the end of the year, and somehow I talked The producer of the show into putting me on the air to talk about the experience, and the next thing I knew I had more than 100 people in rolled in my online coaching program and I have never looked back. George Nori is one of the most talented interviewers and insightful radio personalities I have ever met, and he is a true professionals voice artist, showing up night after night after night for years and years and years all around the globe and dealing with such a diverse collection of subjects that it would blow your mind if you knew the full extent of what he has done. Check out his show and study his technique if you want to observe true master speaker.

DAVE NASSANEY became the most unlikely hero in my community of magic messengers when he decided he was going to book himself on 10 TV shows and accomplish that and more before he even showed up for his *Celebrity Launchpad* implementation event. I was very tough on him while I coached him during the webinars, but to Dave's credit he did what I told him and booked himself on 14 appearances to promote his book for caregivers and his podcast "Dave the caregivers caregiver radio show", and now he is out there burning his chops and learning how to be a great guest. I am most impressed by his business like attitude of just making the calls and getting it done, and I am gratified to have a man of his capabilities and potential who is willing to execute my instructions and coaching and make me look good. If you are a caregiver you over to yourself to listen to his radio show and buy his book at www.davenassaney.com

LIAT GATT

was one of my very first superstar success stories, and has gone on to appear on television all across America and become an international knitting expert speaker around the world. I met Liat at the Publicity seminar we both attended back in 2010, and even though she had never been on TV yet, I knew that her beautiful personality and knitting expertise would do great on TV, and was happy to have her in one of the first *Celebrity Launchpad* classes, where she got booked by almost everyone. If you need a speaker for your crafts conference or your knitting event you could not do any better than Liat. If you are interested in learning how to knit as a hobby or for therapeutic purposes, go straight to **www.KnitFreedom.com**

SEAN KING is one of my favorite entrepreneurs in the world, and one of the best speakers I know, especially in the world of home-improvement. Sean was very funny in that he worried about his prospects for success at *Celebrity Launchpad* or in *Business Expert Forum at Harvard Faculty Club,* but I'm happy to say that he is one of the

most outstanding case studies we have produced with both of those experiences. Sean has done more than 30 television shows including Fox Los Angeles, and he is making all kinds of money by leveraging his TV and Harvard speaking appearances with postcards and other speaking gigs. He really is a uniquely entertaining speaker because of his physicality and commitment to rehearsing and performing as an entertainer should. If you need a great real estate speaker or if you have a house that needs renovation in southern New England you should definitely check out Sean King.

www.RiskFreeGuaranteed.com

SEAN SMITH is a truly inspiring public speaker, and winner of the women networks "North America's next greatest speaker competition" – – which is an astounding feet if you consider the fact that he is not a woman. As a speaker and Coach Sean will inspire you to dig deep and find that moving truth inside of you that will be the kernel that moves others to know like and trust you. As a student in my TV publicity training program, Sean was a superstar because he was such a great speaker and made it look easy to book yourself on television, and then to be a great guest on television as well. I have the utmostRespect for Sean as a speaker and as a speaker coach and appreciate his inspirational role in my life.

SHERMAN RAGLAND is a fellow graduate of the Wharton Business School, and one of the sharpest real estate speakers I know. Sherman runs the real investors Academy where he teaches people how to make money for real by investing in real estate, and it is this community that has made him the great speaker that he is today. He is also one of the smartest marketers I know, especially when it comes to using celebrity attachment and circumstantial Social Proof photos and videos

in social media posts. I learned from him every day both when he speaks and when he markets himself on social media, and I am proud to call him a friend as well as a student and a mentor.

JEFF PEOPLES

is one of the smartest people I have ever met. He provides the software that saves his clients millions and millions of dollars when they mail 5 out of every 10 envelopes delivered by the US Postal Service. Jeff has become one of the most exciting speakers I know, and it is through his commitment to a creating freedom as a speaker as well as his commitment to being the consummate student that he has been able to progressed so rapidly. A luminary angel investor and expert on block chain technology, Jeff Peoples is a superstar speaker that has graced stages at Harvard, at West Point, NASDAQ, Coca-Cola, Microsoft, and I would recommend him to anyone who needs a powerful and thought-provoking entrepreneurial technology speaker that will blow peoples minds with his advanced concepts and down to earth presentation style.

JIMMY FALLON has perfected the nice guy persona to the point where he landed the most coveted job on late-night television as host of *The Tonight Show,* walking in the footsteps of Johnny Carson and Jay Leno. A truly talented performer, comedian, actor, interviewer and singer, Jimmy is like a low-calorie chocolate milkshake that you can drink every single night when you go to bed, enjoy every sip of it, and wake up the next morning feeling good about yourself. I look forward to one day sitting beside him at his desk on *The Tonight Show* and being featured as a guest. This is an honor that every author and speaker should aspire to as Jimmy makes everyone look great!

LEWIS HOWES
built a tremendous intellectual property empire on the back of his ability to speak as a host of "School of Greatness" podcast, which he has built up from nothing to the point where it has made him a

New York Times best-selling author and highly paid professional speaker. If you want to learn a lot about a wide variety of subjects, tune into his podcast for consistent high-quality education delivered by an expert interviewer.

ELLEN DEGENERES has been inspiring and entertaining audiences seemingly forever, and is the undisputed queen of daytime TV talk shows. Her lighthearted charm and likability combined with her comedic genius and innate showmanship have earned her place in the hearts of millions of people around the world. I love how she has discovered so many talents over the years through her willingness to bring unknowns onto her show and debut them in front of the world. A true champion of underdogs and all kinds of people who never would have had a chance to fulfill their destiny were it not for Ellen, television has truly benefited from all that she has given it and all that she has made it be.

OPRAH has been an inspiration for so many millions of people, and today I use her as an example for all of my students to emulate and how to be great on television. A true force for good on this planet and in the society of

ours, Oprah has given so much to so many people, but for anyone who is a speaker or a performer, her ability to communicate and connect with audiences on camera is one that merits deep study and appreciation. She knows how to be powerful on TV she knows how to be subtle on TV she knows how to evoke emotion and connect with audiences and she is someone who I wish was still always on television every single day so that I could watch her every single day.

ELLEN ROHR

"The Plumber's Wife," is one of my greatest success stories and most respected people I know in the world of public speaking. She has decades of experience as an entrepreneur, and when I am unable to accommodate a request to speak at an event, I have gladly referred Ellen to speak in my place. Her message of entrepreneurial empowerment is heartfelt and comes from deep knowledge of "dirty jobs," and she is a tremendous choice for any organization in need of a speaker who can deliver honest expertise from real-world experience.

JOHN LEE DUMAS

is the host of "Entrepreneur on Fire" podcast, and one of the most powerful movers and shakers in the business podcast world. A retired Army veteran, he has single-handedly created his podcast empire through sheer dent of willpower and hard work and commitment to cranking out episode after episode after episode in this new world of iTunes media, to the point where John Lee proudly proclaims his revenues and earnings right on the podcast, and it is very impressive! If you are in entrepreneur you should listen to his podcast, and as a speaker you should listen to his podcast because he always has great guests and his interviews are always amazing.

JUDGE JEANINE PIRRO

is one of the baddest ass truth tellers on television. I admire her so much for her knowledge of what she <u>can</u> do and what would be going too far, that one can only have as a result of being and actual judge and legal expert. My wife and I love watching her opening statements and interviews as much as we enjoy watching anyone on television. Judge Jeanine is a consummate performer as well as a brilliant legal mind and outstanding orator, and anyone who aspires to be great on TV should study the way she speaks and lays out arguments with an entertaining and persuasive flair.

SEAN HANNITY is one of the most rational and sometimes one of the few sane voices on television these days, and his dedication to truth and objective journalism over the past few years has been a tremendous source of solace for me

and many millions of Americans who appreciate his willingness to stand up for what is right in the face of so much opposition from the mainstream media fiction mongers. Mr. Hannity is a tremendous direct to camera television presenter as well as one of the most courageous people on TV. Honestly, I thank God that he is on the air, especially during many of the darkest days of the past few months-long witch-hunt.

DAVE ASPREY is a fellow Wharton business school graduate and a super successful entrepreneur, the mastermind behind the Bulletproof Coffee movement that has swept the world and put him on the biggest TV shows and in the most prestigious newspapers and magazines all around the globe. I had the pleasure of meeting Dave at Genius Network meetings, but I really got to know him because my wife subscribes to and listens to his podcast and I also heard him as a guest on the *Tim Ferris Show*. In addition to him being a brilliant speaker and podcast guest/host, Dave is also a genius when it comes to bio hacking and achieving optimum performance from the human body and mind.

DAVE STRIEGEL is someone who started out as a student of mine and has since evolved into one of my idols. A total low-key soft-spoken actual auto mechanic from Pittsburgh Pennsylvania, Dave showed up in front of me after one of my seminars and told me he had enrolled and that he was an auto mechanic from Pittsburgh. I don't remember this, but he says I told him "I've been waiting for you." It turns out it was true; I was waiting for someone like him to become one of my greatest successes. Dave has gone on to appear on Fox Los Angeles three times, and to speak on the main stage at Mandalay Bay convention center for one of his automotive industry's most prestigious events. This has exploded his auto shop owner coaching business, and propelled him to amazing

 success in his life both professionally and personally with his sweet adorable wife Lisa.

CHALENE JOHNSON is a truly impressive woman who, after a long run of TV infomercial mega-hits, has reinvented herself as a social media superstar. Chalene now regularly speaks on major stages and hosts her own social media marketing events to propel her mentorship empire. Beautiful, smart, and super hard-working, Chalene is the ideal role model and teacher for anyone who wants to make themselves into something out of nothing using the power of social media and content creation elbow grease.

STUART VARNEY is one of my favorite television hosts on Fox, and one of those inspirational people who come to America from a foreign country and end up becoming somebody very very special. I am in awe of people like Mr. Varney who can rise to the top of their industry without the benefit of hometown or local connections. Beyond that, his professional presentation skills and television persona are of the highest level of professional standards and I aspire to one day be a guest on his show.

BRANDON T ADAMS is a young man who is tearing up the world as a speaker, budding television personality, and event producer. I first met Brandon when I was a guest on his fabulous podcast, *Young Entrepreneurs University*, and then he came to *Celebrity Launchpad* and started going on television everywhere, and then he did a reality series with Greg Rollet which has since been nominated for an Emmy award. He produces the Young Entrepreneurs Conventions and there is seemingly no limit for this gorgeous, charismatic, talented, driven, photogenic, mediagenic, smart young man. If you are a young entrepreneur looking for a mentor or someone to emulate, you need to study Brandon T Adams.

RONDI LAMBETH is a true subject matter expert when it comes to credit repair and credit building strategies. He has truly excelled on television and with his stage speaking,

Rondi Lambeth featured speaker for Business Expert Forum at Harvard Facu

Rondi Lambeth

and his ability to leverage opportunities into a credit repair TV series with Grant Cardone TV and to work his way onto big stages with Grant and his posse is truly impressive. On top of that, Rondi is a wonderful human being and a very nice person, and I have nothing but respect, admiration and positive endorsement for him as a speaker — especially as a credit expert. **www.FortressCreditPro.com**

BARBARA KHOZAM one of the most accomplished and successful female speakers I know, she is one of only 16 elite level women in the Toastmasters professional speaking organization, and works

internationally as a paid keynote speaker, with a powerful message of how to deliver outstanding customer service. She is truly an inspiration for anyone who has high standards as speaker.

ZIG ZIGLAR one of the founding fathers of the motivational speaking industry, Zig set the standard for decades as far as the sales training and motivation were concerned. Today you can still take inspiration and learn from one of the greats to his many audio recordings which are available on Amazon.com, and his son **TOM ZIGLER** carries on the tradition of his father at Ziglar.com

"You can have everything in life you want, if you will just help other people get what they want."

- Zig Ziglar

MICHAEL DREW is one of the most interesting speakers you will see on the Seminar circuit. His talk, "The Pendulum," illustrates how our society swings back and forth between extremes, and in this way gives you a window into the future based on what we know has already happened. The Pendulum is one of the most polished, profound, thought-provoking presentations I've ever had the pleasure of attending. Michael Drew is a man whose ideas are worthy of study and whose performance as a speaker is worthy of emulation.

JOHN VROMAN and I met while studying with Michael Port in his "Heroic Public Speaking Graduate Program." John gave a performance to the whole group that I'm sure no one has forgotten. It was "Super-Fantastique!" I came home and retold his story to my wife, and even today she still references Super-Fantastique from time to time, and she wasn't even there! John is one of those speakers who you are lucky to see on the college circuit, and I'm sure will be taking down big paychecks from corporate gigs for many years.

LISA NICHOLS

provides a beacon of hope for her community of primarily women speakers. She has a ferocious personal story and takes no prisoners when she delivers her message. She literally expects people to break down in tears and "fall out" from listening to her story of abuse and personal transformation, and they do. Lisa is one of the most powerful speakers you will have the privilege to see on the circuit today, and always draws passionate crowds into her audience. She has a large community of speakers who attend her trainings and seminars who are rabid fans, and TV host Steve Harvey identifies Lisa as his personal coach.

MANNY FABRIQUER delivers super powerful information about how to get into great colleges and how to go to great colleges for free. A sincere and sincerely great speaker with tons of passion and high levels of performance skills, Manny is always entertaining to watch on stage, and always delivers a great message with profound emotional power. He has tons of great ideas that you will never see from anyone else, and has done such a great job at Harvard and it NASDAQ that his message will also take him to main stage speaking opportunities at Coca-Cola, Microsoft, and many other places in 2018 and beyond. Also an amazing chef, look for his phenomenal cookbook coming out soon for single dads!

Michael Martinez FEATURED SPEAKER Business Expert Forum at Harvard Faculty Club

MIKE MARTINEZ has a passion for helping Honda associates retire with freedom and power, and a long history of Honda automobiles in his own life, and this is probably the secret key to why he is such a successful speaker for this market. If you are anyone who works in the automotive industry and plan on retiring with a pension, you need to go see Mike Martinez speak. If you are financial advisor of any kind, you would do well to study how he skillfully blends personal story with financial advice to deliver highly entertaining and informative presentations that make him tons of money.

COREY PETERSON speaks on the hottest topic in the real estate seminar space, multi-family investments. He specializes in helping people who have been doing single family fix and flips to transition into the far more lucrative wealth building field of multi-family investments. Corey is a very passionate and experienced expert in this investment area, and has made a lot of money for himself and his investors over the years leading Kahuna Investments. Now he is hitting it hard on the circuit with his new multi-family training program, and he is a real speaker to watch with explosive growth. He also happens to be a super smart guy with a gorgeous wife and family and a bad ass motorcycle rider too!

KEVIN FREAM is one of the hottest information technology and cyber security speakers on the circuit today. His MatrixForce organization is a leader in the field, and he is a guy who really knows how to use what other people would consider "handicaps" as a unique advantage for him as a speaker. Kevin has been a superstar speaker at Harvard and at NASDAQ, and I know that he will be speaking at Coca-Cola and Microsoft in 2018, so make sure to get your butt in a seat at one of his upcoming events.

169

TAMI PATZER

created blue ocean territory for herself with a "beyond the bestseller" service she provides for authors. She has helped a lot of my clients become best-

selling authors, to leverage their media and speaking appearances, and she has really broken through as a speaker by accessing her personal stories and willingness to be vulnerable. She is a real mover to watch, I'm grateful to have had her on my stage at Harvard and look forward to hearing her at NASDAQ, Coca-Cola, and Microsoft!

JIM HEAFNER hales from North Carolina where he is the state's leading financial advisor. He has really broken through and pushed his speaking career to new heights at Harvard, West Point, and NASDAQ. He is a frequent expert

guest on TV news & talkshows all across the country, and when you see him speak you should pay careful attention to what makes him so gosh darn likable, because I believe that his knowledge of the financial industry and likability combine as his most powerful secret for success.

KIM CURTIS has really broken through to massive success thanks to her amazing performances on stage at West Point, Harvard, NASDAQ, on TV, and especially in her work in the state of Colorado where she was named one of the States Top 10 financial advisors. Her clients include multiple governors of states, national television personalities, and even cage fighting superstars in the UFC, but she is so super nice and humble that you would never imagine she was such a superstar. What impresses me most about this dynamo speaker is her professionalism and commitment to pushing herself to new heights and new levels of achievement while at the same time maintaining her commitment to her family.

TROY FULLWOOD is a superstar financial speaker who graced our stage at Harvard and did an amazing job at NASDAQ. He is a big guy with a huge heart and an important message for anybody who wants to make money without losing their soul in the process.

JEREMY MATRANGA has a story that will blow your mind and inspire you to make changes in your life that you've been putting off for far too long. He is also a brilliant financial advisor and committed family man. His career as a speaker is on a hockey stick trajectory with

outstanding appearances at Harvard and NASDAQ under his belt, and lots of TV on the horizon. This man has a true commitment to personal development and he's willing to put in the hard work required, so keep your eye on him and get into an audience when he is on stage so that you can take the ride of his success trajectory with him.

DELON LUKOW takes cyber security very very seriously. I'm warning you right now, if you are in the audience when he talks about this topic you are going to be feeling very very scared about how vulnerable your entire life is, and about the bad actors who can ruin everything you are doing so easily. He is a true cyber security expert, and a passionate speaker on this topic. Check out his website and all the celebrities he hangs out with and you will understand why he is moving so fast and going places so rapidly. Delon is a heckuva nice guy and a true dedicated family man, as well as being a really fun speaker to watch.

ALICE BRANTON is a force of nature! It's hard to believe that God could put so much good looks and energy and beauty and personal power into one single person, but that's exactly what he did with her. This woman's effectiveness as a speaker is powered by her devotion and "religious zeal for her topic of healing with energy and with vitamin D. This is a female speaker who has an in Normas future thanks to the great work she has already accomplished at Harvard and NASDAQ and on so many TV shows all across this country.

DR. LALEH SHABAN has blossomed before my eyes like he miraculous flower. Aside from being one of the most successful medical practitioners I have ever met, with an in Normas Lee thriving practice in San Luis Obispo California,

she has become one of the most fantastic and enthusiastic speakers I have ever seen, seemingly from a standing start. Her personal stories will blow your mind, and her deep knowledge and God-given gifts for healing will change your life.

DR. SCOTT DAVIS

is a powerful voice for rational behavior and wellness. An MD who has helped more than 10,000 patients over the course of his 25 year career in medicine, Scott speaks with authority, power, confidence and conviction that only comes from the experience of saving lives. He was one of the most impressive speakers I saw at West Point and again at Harvard, and I look forward to more of him at NASDAQ, Coca-Cola and Microsoft where he will be sharing his vision for Corporate Wellness plans.

VINCE DAVIS has the power to save your family. Anybody who has ever listened to Vince's radio show knows his passion for protecting families against the abuses of child protective services. Big-name celebrities like Brad Pitt and will smith know how far the CPS swap is willing to go to ruin your life, but Vince Davis seems to be one of the few people in the world who has the power and the willingness to do anything about it. Seeing him "preach" on this topic at heart Open my eyes to the importance of his message, but his continued willingness to proselytize about this most evil entity is truly inspirational and if you are a family in need of his help you should seek him out and avail yourself of his wise counsel.

DR. DEBRA SCHREIBMAN is on a rocket ride of personal and professional transformation for her life, and this will overflow into the lives of anyone lucky enough to become one of her patients. She has a true gift and passion for functional medicine, healing people through education and scientific analysis of what's

really wrong with them instead of just dealing with symptoms. Her appearance at Harvard and NASDAQ were both eye-opening and transformative for everyone in the audience, and if you have an opportunity to see or hear her speak, you can trust that it will result in you having a fuller understanding of how to live a healthy life and take your physical, emotional, and spiritual wellbeing to the next level.

ALF TEMME has been a pioneer in the field of high impact training for decades, the originator of the Raam apparatus (which Tony Robbins owns five of) has made him an exercise and fitness innovator and leader for decades. His power as a speaker comes from his deep knowledge of this topic and his commitment to showing

up Strong for his audience and himself.

TOM MACK will most likely surprise the heck out of you when you hear him speak. His amazing stories of

entrepreneurship getting back to his youth will inspire and connect with you, and his use of technology for the generation and reducing and entrepreneurs bloodletting at events will help you take your business to much higher levels. He is an extremely hard worker and dedicated speaker who is performances I have enjoyed immensely at Harvard and it NASDAQ and on television, and it's another real up-and-coming voice on the speaker circuit today.

SANDI MASORI was one of my earliest breakout success stories, appearing on ***The Today Show*** only three months after attending *Celebrity Launchpad*. Her commitment to television celebrity has earned her recurring appearances on Fox Los Angeles and national television shows, and she is one of the most exciting and entertaining TV celebrities to watch because of her high energy and colorful work with balloons! She speaks frequently at conferences and events and has brilliant mind for what it takes to make money as a balloon entrepreneur. Check out Sandi at www.BalloonExpert.com

STEVE HARVEY — king of all daytime talk show hosts on television today, Steve is an inspiration for so many people and for so many reasons. He is a person you have enormous respect for because you can see in his face that he has worked extremely hard for

everything that he has today and that he deserves everything he has, and all the success he has achieved. He is also in normal sleep likable, and the kind of person that you want to have like you, the kind of person that you want to call your friend. In addition to being a talented comedian and performer, Steve is also a tremendous motivational speaker, and you have probably seen his motivational speech "jump" on Facebook video or on YouTube. Today, if you can appear on the Steve Harvey show you have made it to the top of the television world, and for that reason alone you should be watching and studying everything that this man does and shares with us on TV.

MICHAEL PORT is one of the coolest guys I know in the speaker/expert/ seminar world, (and I feel the exact same way about his lovely, adorable and brilliantly intelligent, super-talented wife **AMY PORT**.) Really smart, really successful, with a personality that is at once genuine and 100% Teflon,

this is a coach and speaker that I have learned a tremendous amount from, and I aspire to be more like in every way. He is a true subject matter expert in that he has been on all sides of the camera and on tons of stages around the world, and also has tremendous skills and experience as a coach, director, producer, and author of best-selling books.

I have participated in their large Heroic Public Speaking seminars, and then went on to participate in their rigorous and intensive graduate program, and I have done private coaching with Michael too, and I have nothing but the highest positive remarks and level of respect for Michael and his wife Amy, who runs the live events with him. The most impressive thing about Michael and Amy is that in all of my many dealings with them over a long period of time, I have never seen them lose their cool even once. These two are consummate professionals of the highest caliber, and I 100% endorse everything that they are doing with all levels of Heroic Public Speaking.

TONY ROBBINS

is probably the speaker who inspires more people to be more, do more, have more, and become better speakers than anyone else in the world. He is a force of nature, and if you have never attended his

live events you owe it to yourself to carve out some time and money to give this gift of personal transformation and personal development to yourself. He is unique as a speaker and trainer in the world because of the tremendous personal power and seemingly infinite amounts of experience he has put himself through in the seminar and personal development industry. An Idol, a legend, a force for good, and an example to be emulated by everyone who aspires to be a great speaker and performer.

DANIEL HALL is one of the most interesting mentors I have ever had, and also one of the most interesting speakers I have ever seen. He comes out of the Tom and Tiant school of low key persona come and although he is a brilliant and super intelligent attorney, author, lawyer, man, and coach, his performance and delivery is deliberately "un-slick." I have studied with him on the topic of webinars, and I have done a co-venture with him, and everything that I've done with him has been a positive experience and profitable. He is tremendously industrious and cranks out tons of interesting and useful content through his webinars, and I recommend that you study with him and invest with him with full expectation that you will get great value from everything you do with him.

MJ JENKINS

has transformed herself from someone with a dream into someone who now has a career as an International spokesperson on behalf of the American Cancer Society, bringing awareness to the world about breast cancer. She is one of my greatest success stories, having appeared on 50+ television interviews all around the world, including National appearances in south Africa, and on multiple hits in Los Angeles. MJ is a great friend and a person with tons of heart and passion to help women overcome the challenges of breast cancer.

JORDAN HARBINGER

hosts one of the most successful podcasts on iTunes, *"The Art of Charm."* I met Jordan at Michael Port's Heroic Public Speaking seminar, where we became friends, and I was thrilled to have him join us as a *Business Expert Forum at Harvard Faculty Club* main-stage speaker, where he delighted and enthralled the audience with his entertaining and fascinating stories. He is a tremendous interviewer and speaker, and I have nothing but the highest respect for him in his stage performance abilities and everything he has done on iTunes.

BRENDON BURCHARD

truly was responsible for opening my eyes to the income and lifestyle possibilities of being a guru/expert in what he termed the "experts industry." I was lucky enough and smart enough to have made the wise decision to invest a lot of money in his *Empire Group* mastermind program early on in my career as a speaker, and as a result I got to observe and study Brendon's performance and business structure extensively and at close range. I do believe that his strongest abilities and the greatest factor of his success is his strengths as a speaker and performer and storyteller. But overall, the guy is marketing genius. I am most grateful to Brendon for his example and the path he forged for me and so many others to live lives of total freedom and abundance as speakers and expert coaches.

LES BROWN delivers one of the
most powerful personal inspirational stories you will ever have the good fortune to receive. Les is undoubtedly one of the all-

time greatest speakers to ever grace the stage, and has inspired countless speakers to want to follow in his footsteps. A fiercely passionate and driven leader in the industry, if you want to see what one of the all-time greatest professional speakers looks like and performs like, you need to get your butt into a seat at one of his performances. This man is truly a legend and lives up to that reputation every time he opens his mouth. His "hospital gown" video is the best, most moving performance I've ever seen — I actually cried.

OREN KLAFF is a master of pitching business deals and I am a proud graduate of his *"Pitch Anything"* training program. He is a super smart guy and a brilliant business mind, especially when it comes to speaking about very big dollar business ideas, and especially about crafting a Big Idea. I am particularly impressed with the way that Oren has used his speaking and training activities as a way to generate high priced consulting clients. This is perfect execution of what being a VIP speaker is truly about.

RICK STEELE is an extremely passionate entrepreneur and speaker who we were privileged to have with us on the main stage in *Business Expert Forum at Harvard Faculty Club* 2015, where we bestowed upon him the Humanitarian Award for his work in eradicating dangerous and deadly cords on window blinds, which results in the death of so many innocent and unfortunate children and animals every year.

TED MCGRATH is a tremendous speaker, entrepreneur, and coach whom I had the great pleasure to meet way back in the beginning days of my career as a speaker and expert, while attending *Experts Academy.*

Today he is one of the most successful and highest priced entrepreneurial coaches working in the business. I have personally watched him enroll multiple $100,000 clients at a live event — it was incredibly impressive. I know several of his clients who are getting massive results through their work with Ted. He's also an extremely driven and talented performer, continually refining and developing his own one-man show.

JOYCE GIOIA delivers more dedication and commitment to her craft as a speaker than any other grandmother working in the business today. Still going strong with Multi-decades of experience as a paid professional speaker, she is one of my favorite people and one of my all time greatest success stories for TV publicity training, as she was able to propel herself onto ***The TODAY Show*** roughly 6 months after her *Celebrity Launchpad.* She is a brilliant futurist, *USA Today*'s first Road Warrior of The Year, and I am proud to call her a friend, mentor, and someone I look to for insight and guidance whenever I can.

GENE GUARINO is one of the most consummate professionals in the real estate speaking arena, and his unique approach to educating entrepreneurs about assisted living facilities and how to create residential assisted living empires is the hottest ticket in the industry and creating huge opportunities for those lucky enough to find themselves in a room with Gene Guarino as their expert coach. I was very fortunate to be invited to speak at one of his Residential Assisted Living Academy events, and some of my favorite people are members of his community.

GARRET J WHITE leads one of the most successful movements occurring in the personal development and transformation space today: Wake Up Warrior. A charismatic, passionate, and persuasive speaker,

coach, and visionary, Garrett and I both came out of those early days in Brendon Burchard's Experts Academy. Today he has crystallized a vision and community, transforming hundreds and thousands of men and families into more engaged, effective, and successful Entrepreneurs, Business people, men, couples, and families. I have been particularly impressed with his use of documentary style filmmaking and his authoritative, biblical $99 Black Book to propagandize his message and promote his unique movement.

NATE LIND leads a high status entrepreneurial conference in Aspen called Adsum, at which I had the privilege to speak for the first time in 2017. High-level high-net-worth individuals in

attendance. He is a powerful messenger for his masculine men's movement and his beard products, and we were privileged to have him grace our stage in 2017 at Harvard.

EBAN PAGAN is one of the most brilliant minds in the personal development, marketing and seminar industries. I had the great fortune of attending his *METAMIND* event in Miami back in 2013, and was forever influenced by the brilliant format and collection of thought leaders and industry leaders he assembled. He has a low key style of delivery driven by his superior intelligence and seemingly deep pockets, and that level of not needing anything or not seeking any approval from anyone gives him tremendous power as a speaker and a host because he can be so authentic and deliver what he really feels to be his truth. This man really knows how to make money in the personal development and seminar space, and his legion of fans and followers worship him and have nothing but the best things to say about what he delivers and the value they get.

JOE POLISH

delivers one of the most beguiling forms of expert presentations you will ever encounter. With a pronounced disdain for any kind of pretense or formality, Joe focuses on delivering humor and time-tested experience-traveled entrepreneurial lessons from his many many years working in the seminar industry and as a marketing expert. Another long time protégé of Dan Kennedy, Joe's **Genius Network** is one of the most successful entrepreneurial communities I have ever invested in, and an inspiration to me as a student of his genius. Joe has taught me many things, foremost being the importance of delivering humor in presentations and of having more fun in everything you do. Joe is also the co-host, with Dean Jackson, of the *I Love Marketing* Podcast, one of the most influential entrepreneurship podcasts on the Internet, and a true source of endless educational bounty for anyone who wants to have better marketing in their business.

DR. CHARLES WEBB is a singular force of charisma and personal power who has done more to help doctors earn what they deserve in today's precarious medical and insurance environment than anyone else in America. His Freedom Practice Coaching organization and his work as a speaker who trains doctors to have more impact on their communities and on their practices, continues to be a revolutionary force in the way medicine is delivered in this country. Dr. Webb delivers his message with power and authority, and it is a privilege to be associated with his organization and to contribute to the education and training of his clients. I sincerely appreciate his razor sharp business mind and his encouragement to provide opportunity amongst his community.

JOEL BAUER is undoubtedly one of the most influential speakers and speaker-trainers working in the industry over the past several decades. He is a consummate professional speaker and sales authority, and his mark can instantly be seen stamped on his students and protégés, of which I am proud to call myself one. There are few people that I would trust to reorganize and rework my presentation, and I am happy that I have hired Joel for private consultation at top dollar and with profound impact on my work. I am always happy to have the opportunity to watch this master wild his skills in front of any audience, as he delivers volumes of instruction sheerly by the example of his speaking. If you want to learn how to make more money as a speaker, *study Joel Bauer.*

DR. PETER OSBORNE passionately delivers his message against grain wherever he can, and evangelizes as a marketing expert for medical professionals. He is a

passionate entrepreneur and marketing expert for healers and medical practitioners of all kinds, and his depth of knowledge and commitment to delivering marketing education to his community is of the highest level and integrity. I was privileged to bestow upon Dr. Osborne the Mentorship Award of *Business Expert Forum at Harvard Faculty Club* in 2017, and recommend that any medical professional interested in raising the results of their marketing attend his conference in Houston.

IVAN MISNER founded and leads the world's preeminent networking organization, BNI, and has grown it into an international powerhouse and force for good through referrals and professional development of it's members. I have had the great privilege to here Ivan's message and witness his professional presentations twice at Wizards Academy (through Alex Mandossian's Pathfinders Mastermind,) and always come away with priceless gems of personal and professional wisdom as well as an appreciation for this man's Journey and evolution as an entrepreneur and professional speaker, generating untold millions through his presentations and through the impact of those presentations on the lives of his members. Always high-value, always entertaining, always worth your time and effort to get into an audience for one of Ivan's presentations.

SUZANNE SOMERS was kind enough to grace my stage at the 2017 installment of *Business Expert Forum at Harvard Faculty Club*. She was a total delight to work with as a consummate professional in her storytelling, poise, and sophisticated presentation as an entertainer delivering an important message about health and success as an entrepreneur. At times while I was sitting next to her on the stage I was absolutely *awestruck* by her physical beauty, and other times I was blown away by the depth of her insight and maturity as a business person and performer. Suzanne is an inspiration as an entertainer and demonstrates the power of professional speakers to impact & influence the world.

CAITLYN JENNER embodies the ultimate accomplishments as a superstar celebrity, and I am thrilled to be interviewing her for *Business Expert Forum at Harvard Faculty Club* 2018. To me, no one has accomplished as many outstanding publicity triumphs as Caitlyn, and I bought the copy of Vanity Fair magazine with her on the cover intending to frame it and

study it for the rest of my life as the ultimate publicity coup of all-time and all history. Her courage and personal power both astound and inspire me to fulfill on my unique personal mission and I am delighted by the prospect of sharing her with my community in the months ahead.

CRAIG DUSWALT has created a marketing empire buy harnessing rock'n roll showbiz principles as his special niche to deliver entertaining business education seminars and coaching to his clients. Having had the privilege to speak at his *Rockstar Marketing Boot Camp*, I got to witness firsthand the genius of his program and curriculum to transform new and advanced marketing students alike into more successful entrepreneurs, and I am constantly appreciative of how much entertainment value he packs into everything that he does as a seminar leader and as a speaker. He's also a great dad and family man.

"CAPTAIN LOU" EDWARDS is one of the most interesting speakers that I know in the expert seminars industry. He uniquely focuses on specialty cruises that he organizes for specific industries and sectors, and within this niche he is at the top of his game. My favorite part of Capt. Lou is his consummate professionalism and skills as a speaker who understands the value of entertainment and the power of "shtick" to enhance entertainment value. Beginning with his costume, continuing with his corny jokes and phraseology, Capt. Lou knows exactly what he's doing exactly how to keep an audience with him and having a great time. He is also a very Pleasant and fun guy to hang around, and has maintained the highest reputation over many years in industry.

DAVEN MICHAELS delivers a powerful message of liberation and empowerment for entrepreneurs through his smart outsourcing services. He is the *New York Times* best-selling author of "Outsource Smart," and is truly a unique speaker, author, entrepreneur who embodies his message of living the power of a laptop lifestyle — and delivers many of the resources required to emulate his lifestyle through his 1,2,3 Products and solutions. Daven truly understands the power of entertainment, and delivers it with his entrepreneurial educational message when he speaks, on many of the biggest and most prestigious stages around the world on a regular basis. He's also a really smart and a really nice guy, with a great heart and devotion to his family and inner circle of clients.

ALEX JEFFREYS has delivered pound for pound more success stories than any other coach working in the experts industry today. A brilliant entrepreneur and business thinker, Alex blows me

away with his willingness to take risks, invest in himself, reinvent himself, and make money in ways that no one else is doing. He is a true master of webinars and online coaching, and a charismatic speaker who has been gracious enough to share his message with my audience at Harvard, and two have invited me to share my message with his audience. Alex and his partner Adam Davies are two entrepreneurs whom I am proud to call friends and endorse with my highest approval.

JEFFERSON SANTOS delivers mentorship, inspiration, and leads a giant community of money-making world-traveling entrepreneurs through his World Ventures organization. I have witnessed firsthand how hard he works and what a tremendous salesman and sales trainer he truly is. With a downline organization numbering in the many *thousands*, you would think Jefferson would be retired permanently to some tropical beach with his family, but he continues to be a believer and a fantastic example of how important it is to keep driving and pushing forward as an entrepreneur. Jefferson regularly speaks on stage in **arenas** at his training events, and knows how to move an audience and get rooms of people motivated, whether it be 2 people in a hotel suite or 20,000 people in a stadium — both of which I have witnessed with my own eyes. He is one of the smartest and hardest working entrepreneurs I know, and I have nothing but the highest level of respect and endorsement for everything that Jefferson Santos touches. $$$ + ✈ + 🚢 = Jefferson Santos

JEFF MOORE was standing in the middle of a crowd at *Experts Academy* when I first laid eyes on him, and I was immediately attracted and sought him out as a friend, colleague, and Mentor. Whenever it is possible for me to attend his *Thursday Night Boardroom* mastermind meeting, I will usually drive an hour and a half in heavy Los Angeles traffic to make it happen. Jeff is one of the most intelligent, experienced, and giving people I have met in the experts industry, and the community he has created with TNB is one of my favorite organizations that I belong to, and has resulted in tremendous professional and personal growth for me both as a speaker and as an entrepreneur. Jeff knows amazing people around the world, and his leadership belies more skills as a speaker then he even knows. If you have a chance to attend one of Jeff's events you should grab it, and if you have an opportunity to be mentored through Jeff's entrepreneurial speaking/coaching you should consider yourself fortunate, especially if you are in the food or food service industries.

BRIAN TRACY always sets the example for me. Many times I have found myself in a situation where I've asked myself "What would Brian Tracy do?" Then, whatever I think Brian Tracy would do, that's why I do. This man is one of the most professional and experienced public speakers and motivational speakers who has ever worked in the modern era. Mild-mannered yet ultimately impactful, his deceptively

low key demeanor is the result of many decades of studied evolution as a professional speaker and leading authority on business, sales, motivation, and public speaking. If you want to study a consummate pro, and are looking for a standard by which to measure your own professionalism, you could not do better than to use Brian Tracy as your model.

DIANA BOOHER was kind enough to share her brilliant thoughts with me on the topic of "strong starts for a presentation" several years ago when I was first beginning my journey as a speaker and expert, and I have never forgotten what she said, and always use her teachings in every presentation

that I do. She is a member of the Speakers Hall of Fame, and a highly paid communications consultant and best-selling author on the topic of communication, which has resulted in a multi decade career as a public speaker and Communications expert. If you are looking for a seriously high-level expert to guide your corporate communications, and have the budget for her level of expertise, you would be fortunate to hire her as you're coach or consultant.

MICHAEL GERBER

has had one of the most profound influences on the entrepreneurial World of any speaker still working today. His eMyth series of books, products, and seminars is deservedly omnipresent in the entrepreneurial community, and his work as a speaker has been one of the driving forces for the success of this message. He is a brilliant businessman and a very generous soul, who was gracious enough to share the story of his unique trademarked hat with me on video at a conference recently. Click **www.is.gd/GerberHat** to watch the video.

MATT LOOP and I met when we were both speakers at Peter Osborn's medical marketing conference, where Matt presented his social media expertise to the group and raked in a huge new gaggle of clients who need his special brand of social media **savoir-faire** designed to enhance the impact of medical professional practices. He is a brilliant entrepreneur and marketer, and an entertaining speaker who motivates people to take action, and delivers a message that students and clients can understand and easily implement into their business. I value Matt as one of the most outstanding speakers in *Business Expert Forum at Harvard Faculty Club* 2017, and have nothing but the highest respect for his ability to deliver on what he promises, as a Speaker, a JV partner, and as a mentor.

JACK CANFIELD has probably trained more trainers than anyone working today. He is responsible for my initial pursuit of television as a means to differentiate myself in my career in the marketplace, and he has delivered equally profound mentorship to countless other speakers and experts all around the world. Jack is one of the most intelligent and

compassionate individuals you will ever meet, and he has total expertise in dealing with people and delivering breakthrough results for any kind of coach, speaker, trainer, or consultant. If you want to invest money and work with the top level coach for speakers working in the 21st-century, you will be lucky to get into one of his classes or seminar rooms.

SCOTT SMITH is the host of one of my all-time favorite podcasts, *"The Daily Boost — Motivation to Move"* — and has one of the very best voices you could ever listen to if you want to improve your performance as a speaker on radio or podcast or any medium that focuses on the sound of your voice alone. He has been delivering inspirational broadcasts for years and years, has built a huge audience for his unique style of motivation and inspiration, and I am in awe of his abilities as a professional speaker and performer.

PENG JOON will lull you into a false sense of security with his boyish charm and good looks, but underneath that disarming countenance lies one of the most successful salesman to ever set foot on a seminar stage. Peng has the intelligence to hire the best coaches and do exactly what they tell him to do, being both a protégé of Joel Bauer and myself. I am proud to hold him up as an example of what is possible for anyone to accomplish if they really want it and if they set their minds to it, as this young man has become one of the breakaway success stories in the world of public speaking and selling from the stage. If you want to watch a truly masterful salesman at work, moving an audience from a cold start to the point of purchase in mere minutes, plunk down your money and take a well deserved lesson from the young Jedi Master himself.

AARON YOUNG is one of the most selfless messengers you will find in any seminar room. His personal story of persecution and prosecution for crimes he did not commit is powerful and moving, and

primes the audience for his unique message of corporate asset protection. If you are the owner of an LLC or Corporation and do not know about Aaron Young and his offerings, you are at risk of losing everything, and must check out what he has to offer at www.LaughlinUSA.com

LT. GENERAL RUSSEL HONORÉ was a true gentleman in every moment that I interacted with him during my adventures creating *Leadership Speakers Academy at West Point*. A consummate professional and amazing presenter as a speaker, his message and delivery of that message stands out as being the best speaker I have ever paid for to grace my stage. If you are looking for an amazing speaker for your corporate event, someone who can deliver star power, authority, experience, and an entertaining, professional presentation for any level of audience, including the highest levels of executives and C-suite thinkers, you could do far worse than to hire General Honoré as your man. He was always available to go the extra mile for me in every interaction, and I sincerely appreciate who and what he is to the speaker industry and for this planet.

JOHN RANKINS

was kind enough to appear as the final speaker at the 2017 Harvard thought leader conference we hosted with Suzanne Somers, and he blew away everyone with his impassioned and entertaining heartfelt presentation. A brilliant entrepreneur who has created a massive sales organization in Asia, John is transforming the lives of thousands who would otherwise be impoverished, but through their association with him have become abundant. He is a genius sales trainer and expert on building sales organizations, and much of that comes from his experience and expertise as a speaker, leader, and motivator of people. His personal story of resilience is both inspirational and instructive, and anyone who has the privilege to hear him speak and share his life experiences is in for a massive treat. This is also one man who understands the power of marketing and celebrity positioning, and for whom I have nothing but respect.

LISE GOTTLIEB:

The E-Commerce Queen of Denmark is a very smart and hard-working up-and-coming speaker, with beauty and tremendous passion for personal growth, she is a great example of making things happen by sheer force of will.

MICHELE SCISM is a super smart business coach and a super-powerful speaker who knows how to use emotional storytelling to wallop her audience. I've been thrilled to feature her on the main stage of *Business Expert Forum at Harvard Faculty Club,* and put her up as the first speaker of the day to make sure we got off to a tremendously strong start — and she delivered. Watch her on TV, and get into her audience to experience the raw power of this great woman speaker for yourself.

BERNIE DOHRMAN

is a very talented and moving speaker who knows how to use his personal story to create connection and trust with an audience. As the founder of CEO Space International, Bernie hosts multiple

conferences every year for all levels of entrepreneurs who are seeking to expand their skills, knowledge, connections, and many times obtain funding for their projects. He brings in many of the top speakers in the world as his faculty at CEO Space, so he has had the opportunity to work with and learn from the greatest performers in multiple disciplines and industries over many years, which you can see in the way he presents in front of audiences of all sizes.

PERRY BELCHER is a co-founder of Digital Marketer, and one of the main presenters at the Traffic & Conversion Summit. He is an investor and well-known sales strategist specializing in authority marketing, channel selling, and email deliverability, and to me, he is like the "grown-up" on the stage next to his boyish partner Ryan Deiss. He presents a very mature, accomplished and super-solid persona on stage, and nothing he does feels in the least bit "produced" or "performed" — he's just a guy up there on stage in front of 4,000 people talking about stuff that he knows will make them more money.

ROBERT ALLEN has been inspiring and educating audiences on stage and through his numerous New York Times bestselling books for many decades. A very polished and experienced speaker and performer on the topic of wealth

creation, Robert has been an inspiration to me for nearly 2 decades, and it is always a thrill to watch him speak.

TAI LOPEZ

is someone I admire greatly because he has created his entire fame and persona essentially by running innovative infomercials on the Internet. This has given him a

tremendous amount of opportunity to perform in front of cameras, and has allowed him to become a very powerful and persuasive speaker on video, which in turn has earned him millions of dollars and made him into a bona-fide internet celebrity — especially for his enormous audience of millennial Internet YouTubers and Facebookers. He is a brilliant marketer and an outstanding video performer worthy of study and emulation, with a super-hot podcast.

MATT LEITZ is the powerhouse performer behind boardgames.com, and one of my all-time favorite *Celebrity Launchpad* graduates. He is tremendously fun to watch on television, and conveys enormous passion and enthusiasm for boardgames in his many television appearances and demonstrations of fun new games you can try with your family. If you really want to watch a speaker and performer whose fun-quotient is infectious and adorable, check out Matt.

BRAD LEA is the genius mastermind behind Lightspeed VT, powering the online training programs of Tony Robbins, Grant Cardone, Zig Ziglar, *Shark Tank's* Damon John, and many many others. He is also "dropping bombs" on his video podcast and as a speaker on stages including the mega-monster 10X Growth Con orchestrated by Grant Cardone. Brad has only recently started making the moves to come out of the shadows of his superstar clients and to promote his own personal brand, and with his enormous personal power and dynamic, charismatic personality it will be hugely fun to watch his trajectory of growth.

STEPHAN SPENCER hosts *The Optimized Geek Podcast* and is a frequent speaker on his topics of SEO Optimization and Google Power Searching. This guy is one pleasant surprise after another, with power and charisma you would never

expect from a geek, and he has a really super-cool personality. He is a brilliant thinker, a very smart business man, and an esteemed graduate of *Celebrity Launchpad* who also happens to be married to a gorgeous Love Goddess!

Col. BUZZ ALDRIN really surprised everyone in *Leadership Speakers Academy at West Point* — he was an *AMAZING* Speaker. I asked his advice on how we could all be better speakers: "Get better writers!" He also told us he took the first selfie (spacewalking!) and used "staged photo opportunities" early on in his career as a military pilot.

HARVEY MACKAY wrote one of the all-time greatest business books, *Swim With The Sharks Without Getting Eaten Alive*, and the guy is a seriously great professional speaker too!

He has so many years of experience in the business world, and has made so many professional speaking appearances promoting his book and sharing his knowledge, and you just can't replace experience! Seriously check him out if you get a chance — he's a very generous spirit and a wise soul.

ROBIN ROBERTS anchors *Good Morning America*, and is one of the most gracious people I have ever met in show-biz. She overcame a very public bout with breast cancer, and the humility of that experience shines through in her kindness, how nice she is, and what a mature and smart person she is. If you ever get a chance to attend a live taping of GMA you will learn many lessons from Robin about how to be a true pro on set at a Top TV Show — or anywhere.

PETER DIAMANDIS must be the smartest guy in the entire world. To see him speak is to get educated. He is on the cutting edge of everything, knows everything and everyone, and always speaks about such expansive ideas —

somehow managing to keep it all on a level that anyone can understand. A true genius speaker.

DEAN JACKSON is like a comet — you know they're out there but it's very hard to actually spot one in person. This guy is the co-host of one of the biggest business podcasts on iTunes, *I Love Marketing*, and yet I

have very rarely been able to see him speak in person. A special treat indeed, and worthy of the effort. Super Smart, very successful, especially about Books, Real Estate & Marketing. You're more likely to see him on video — worth it!

GAIL TRAUCO came through *Celebrity Launchpad* a few years ago and has been on an absolute tear ever since. She has appeared on nearly 50 live TV segments all across the country, and with her beguiling southern drawl she is a very popular return guest! She is

a Grief Counselor by trade, but she is also a very authentic evidentiary psychic medium, and I have personally witnessed old Spanish speaking dead people communicating to their loved ones *through* her — a truly awe-inspiring experience. Supernaturally powerful speaker!

ARIANNA HUFFINGTON delivers a beguiling presentation filled with smart ideas and utterly feminine presence and delivery. She is a rare breed of woman who truly knows how to be very feminine and very powerful at the same time. I've seen her talk on the topic of sleep and rest, and the power of her performance is even more compelling considering the fact that she is a non-native English speaker and has a considerable accent that actually *enhances* every word she says, and makes her somehow sound *smarter*. Non-Native English speakers should especially model her.

DAYMOND JOHN speaks with softness and subtlety in his voice that belies his position of wealth and power as an original and principal Shark on the hit series *Shark Tank*. A super-smart entrepreneur, brand builder, and TV Celebrity, he has gained massive experience delivering entertainment that

educates business people, and he delivers his wisdom in a manner that makes you just LIKE him and want him to like you. Truly worthy of studying, if only to experience his powers of attraction and likability first hand.

DAN SULLIVAN has been a professional speaker and coach for more than 40 years, and this man knows a lot about business and success. During my 2 years of membership in Genius Network, 3 of the Top 10 Lessons that I learned from that experience were direct teachings of Dan Sullivan.

1. **Vacation more.** As entrepreneurs, we need time to recharge and refresh ourselves, as well as down-time to allow creative inspirations to enter our minds.

2. **Vacation before your big events;** prepare yourself to be awesome and to be rested and ready for the hard work.

3. **Do five things every quarter to make your customers and prospects think you are fascinating.**

Dan's main theme in his coaching is that we should only be doing the "Thing" that we do best, and everything else should be delegated to other people. I know a lot of very smart entrepreneurs who have been members of his ***Strategic Coach*** programs, many of them for many many years. This man really knows his way around a platform, and anyone can learn from him about business, about life, and about speaking.

Celebrity Launchpad

&

Prestige Speaking

Opportunities

+

Other Sophisticated

Personal Brand

Transformation Experiences

Available ONLY with

Clint Arthur

>>>>>>>>>>>> > > > > >

YOU CAN BE THE ONLY POSSIBLE CHOICE for CUSTOMERS & PROSPECTS with STATUS MARKETING

GUARANTEED:

YOU SPEAK AT NASDAQ

YOU SPEAK AT HARVARD

CELEBRITY ATTACHMENT

CELEBRITY SIZZLE REELS

CELEBRITY EXPERT POSITIONING

CELEBRITY SPEAKER POSITIONING

ABC NBC CBS FOX TV APPEARANCES

WORLD'S GREATEST MEDIA TRAINING

7-FIGURE SPEAKER-TRAINING & MENTOR

BUSINESS STORY CREATION/DEVELOPMENT

ABOUT

THE AUTHOR

CLINT ARTHUR's

Celebrity Launchpad transformation experiences &

Prestige Speaking Events for Thought-Leaders

are the hottest tickets in Expert Marketing &
Personal Development

www.ClintArthur.TV

CLINT ARTHUR is the world's top expert at creating Celebrity, Authority, and Expert Positioning with **LOCAL TV & "Prestige Speaking**." Since 2012 Clint has taught more than 1000 Authors, Speakers, Coaches, and Entrepreneurs how to deploy his proven, repeatable "Magic Messenger Formula" for booking free TV appearances which they have used to book themselves on 3624+ ABC NBC CBS FOX & CW News & Talk shows, including *Good Morning America, the TODAY Show, Dr. Oz,* CNN, etc. Clint's meteoric ascent in the Expert Industry earned him Dan Kennedy's *GKIC Info-Marketer of The Year* award, and industry recognition as the top Media Trainer in Hollywood.

BOOKS by CLINT

What They Teach You at The Wharton Business School

Break Through Your Upper Limits on TV

Break Through Your Fear of Public Speaking on Local TV

The Last Year of Your Life

The Greatest Book of All Time

The Income Doubler

Accounting/Bookkeeping Freedom for Men/Women

Kickstarter Superstar Success Secrets Revealed

The Last Lecture for Entrepreneurs & Authors

Daddy Loves You

The Presidents Code

21 Performance Secrets of Donald Trump

Performance

AVAILABLE ON AMAZON.COM

SPEAKING GAME SCORE CARD

1) Volume:

2) Speed:

3) Melody:

4) Sustain:

5) Pause:

6) Hand Gestures:

7) Energy:

8) Costume:

9) Status Language:

10) Facial Expressions:

11) Teeth:

12) Setting:

13) SING!

14) Rhyme:

15) Act-Outs:

16) Externalize Inner Monologue:

17) Use Tongue, Eyes, Lips, Nostrils, Feet, Ears:

18) Foreign Language:

19) End Up!

Give Yourself a Point Every Time You Use a Trick – Play by Yourself or with Friends – to 10 or 100 – Have Fun!

CPSIA information can be obtained
at www.ICGtesting.com
Printed in the USA
BVHW08*0422280618
520195BV00009B/174/P